Your Prosperity SuperPower!

Becoming Friends

with Financial Well-Being

and The Law of Attraction

by Graehme Hall

Hermaden Press

©2019

Your Prosperity SuperPower!

Becoming Friends

with Financial Well-Being

and The Law of Attraction

ISBN-13: 978-0-9854284-8-8

ISBN-10: 0-9854284-8-1

Library of Congress Control Number: 2018900704

Hermaden Press
Glen Ellyn, Illinois

www.hermaden.com

First print edition January 2019

Dedicated to you

discovering

you've always had the power

Tap, tap, tap....

And dedicated to Esther and Jerry Hicks

with great love and appreciation

for your work, your path, and your inspiration

Contents

Congratulations on your journey

to understanding and standing in

your power,

to embracing, allowing and aligning

with financial well-being....

Prologue

You are Source energy – God energy, the Force, the Divine, the Creator, Divine Love, call IT what you will – expressing in and through your physical body.

When you have a desire, Source literally becomes that desire. Then Source calls you to the fulfillment of that desire, inspiring you to alignment with it.

There is the place where you are standing vibrationally right now, and the new place where you desire to go.

So you get in your car or airplane, metaphorically speaking, to close the gap and get to this new destination.

Your alignment with reaching this destination – alignment with your Source – will determine how quickly you get there.

There are many, many choices to be made along the way – every thought you think involves a choice, as does every action you take.

The more your choices line up with reaching your destination, the faster you will get there.

As driver, as pilot, you need to focus on where you want to be – not on where you are standing now.

You can't look down at the ground observing where you are, and look forward through your windshield toward where you want to be at the same time. You can't open the vehicle door and look down at the pavement where you are now, and move forward with any great speed.

Source will inspire you, support you, in reaching your desire.

Source is already there. They are providing you with a kind of GPS having already become your desire.

Your emotions are a guidance system, helping you to align with what you have desired to become.

Your emotions provide you with constant feedback about the thoughts you are thinking, and where you are choosing to direct your attention.

If the thought feels good, that thought is in alignment with your desire.

If the thought doesn't feel good, it is out of alignment.

The more it feels good, the greater the alignment.

The worse it feels, the more you are venturing away from an easy path there.

As you know from using actual GPS, there are many alternate routes to reach your desired destination. You can't get it wrong. Some routes simply take longer than others.

Once you have asked to become more, you need to align with who you've become.

Expansion takes many forms. Everyone's path to fulfillment is unique.

Well-being is on your path. But more than that, it is who you are.

You are a powerful creator, fully capable of aligning with well-being in every area of your life. It is the life you came here to live and enjoy.

You have the power. You always have. It's time to remember.

– Hermaden

Chapter 1: Introduction

The universal law of attraction is a topic I have studied many years. I have applied it successfully to most areas of my life. But there was a particular area that kept eluding me: finances. I could not seem to attract prosperity into my life. I worked the exercises and processes that were supposed to bring improvement. I thought, I wrote, I felt, I affirmed, I envisioned. I crawled inside the affirmations and visions until I thought they seemed real. But I could not seem to create more money in my life.

I have the benefit of communicating with a group of wise and loving non-physical teachers that I call Hermaden (pronounced her-mad'den). Some people might call them spiritual guides or angels. They might be seen as extensions of Source, or intermediaries between where we humans are vibrationally and the highest vibrational frequency of Source. They are a collective consciousness, flowing infinite intelligence. They were patient and guided me step by step. They said I was asking as powerfully for understanding and improvement as anyone ever has. But my misunderstanding of prosperity was so deep that real change kept eluding me.

Until.

Until I finally moved to a frequency that was higher, and then they could start sharing with me some of the basic fallacies I had believed and practiced.

Tuning to frequencies is like turning the dial on a radio station. Tuning with your mind. Higher and higher. I knew I needed to tune to a higher frequency, but I couldn't figure it out. Not on this topic.

I have seen others struggle too. Like me, for many years.

It always felt like every time I got close, financial abundance moved further away. It began to feel like I was wearing this rod that kept dangling prosperity in front of me, like the proverbial carrot at the end of a stick. "You want it, but you can't have it." I know that "stick" was my vibration, my frequency. I was projecting an energetic field that was not letting prosperity in.

There were a lot of things I did not understand AT ALL.

Well, now I do.

Not only do I "get it" but the changes in my life support that I am finally "getting it."

I asked Hermaden why it took so many years. Why it was so hard. I was so far away, for so long, from really understanding.

They said that the understanding I have developed can help a lot of other people "get it" too. People who have suffered in ways that did not seem necessary, and were certainly not kind, enjoyable, or fun.

There were aspects of my life that seemed to suffer for a long time, simply because I did not have enough money.

So.

Now I have learned. I have figured it out, with lots of help, from years of asking.

There is no magic pill, or wand to wave.

But consider Dorothy in *The Wizard of Oz*.

Dorothy went on a long journey of discovery before learning to tap together the heels of her red shoes.

Dorothy was looking outside herself for the power to get what she desired, then came to understand the power was within. It was already hers.

Like Dorothy, we have had the power all along.

You have it.

I have it.

We just didn't know we have it.

Now, I do understand that. And I want you to understand too.

That is why I am writing this book.

It is not about the journey I have been on. Relaying those stories won't help you.

It is about the journey you are going on.

It is moving from *where you are* to *where you want to be*.

It is about you.

It is about you becoming audacious enough

to claim who you really are

and the prosperity you deserve.

It is you having, like Dorothy, an experience of awakening.

If you don't like where your finances are in the present, that's okay.

Where you are standing is a temporary place.

You are moving from here, forward. Just like I did.

So don't despair about where you are. You won't be there much longer.

But you must change your life. You must accept that you are the sole offerer of your vibration, your frequency, your energy field. And you have to be willing to change it.

You are the creator of the life you are living.

You – an energetic being – is co-creating with the energies of the Universe. A cooperative Universe.

Now, if you don't believe that the Universe is energy, and you don't believe you are energy, then this book is going to seem crazy and far-fetched to you.

So hopefully you accept that you are energy.

You project an energetic field.

This field is multi-energetic. You are offering many frequencies about different topics. But the range of these frequencies is probably not too large, so they are not too far apart.

You are likely not spending 95% of your life in a joyful, exhilarating place, and feeling shortage of money.

You may be spending 95% of your life in an okay place, or a less-than-okay place.

That is more likely.

You are like the sun.

You offer this field of energy.

You project it, and it travels out into the Universe.

The law of attraction means that like energies attract: like frequencies attract other like frequencies.

Sometimes, frequencies don't line up the way we think they should.

What seems logical at first is not always energetically accurate.

But you will understand more as we move forward.

So.

Come play with me.

Come on a journey with me to greater prosperity.

Your life may not change all at once.

It is usually gradual, like climbing a flight of stairs.

And you will have to work to do it.

As Albert Einstein noted, "No problem can be solved from the same level of consciousness that created it."

If you have been struggling with finances for a while, it means you have some long-standing patterns that need to change.

You can't keep doing what you have been, if it has not been working, and expect change.

You also need to realize that you have some momentum going. Perhaps years, even decades, of momentum.

Shortage is a manifestation of a pattern of energy. That energetic pattern has been offered for a while before it manifests as financial shortage.

Energy precedes form. Always.

So your momentum of shortage began before you started experiencing it.

Now, it doesn't mean it will take you that long to create abundance. Because it won't.

But you wouldn't go jump in front of a fast-moving train and expect it to stop.

You know it can't.

So just allow that it may take a little while for this work to work.

Accept that it will be gradual.

But don't accept that you need to continue to stand where you are if you don't like it.

Don't accept a mediocre result.

You are not mediocre.

You did not come to Earth to create a mediocre life.

The Universe has abundance for you.

Know that.

You can already feel that in your heart.

It's true.

IT'S TRUE!!

You are deserving of a happy, fulfilling life.

You are deserving of abundance.

You are deserving of joy.

Are you ready to open your arms, your heart, and your mind to a better, happier life?

Then let's get started!

Chapter 2: Prosperity Is Already Flowing to Me
(In the beginning of this chapter, Hermaden's remarks are italicized.)

I used to feel like the frequency of abundance and financial prosperity was something outside of me, and I had to learn how to tune to its vibration. Until I could find it, financial well-being would not be mine.

I worked really hard to find it. But I couldn't.

And then Hermaden told me, I was beginning from a false premise.

The stream of abundance is not outside me.

It is flowing THROUGH ME. To me, and through me.

Imagine a stream of light shining down on the top of your head, like a brilliant beam of moonlight.

This is prosperity, Hermaden said.

This is the stream of prosperity that is already flowing to you.

You are born with it.

You don't have to earn it. You don't have to prove your worthiness.

It comes with you here to Earth.

Imagine a tiny newborn, who seems so helpless and dependent on others.

That newborn comes with a stream of abundance, to help attract to the newborn what he or she needs for physical survival.

We are not sending helpless beings to Earth, Hermaden said. *We are sending powerful spiritual beings who are expressing in physical bodies, and come with a strong, dynamic stream of well-being that will help attract, and create, what is needed for survival.*

Haven't you noticed how many adults living in poverty will do their best to feed their children before they feed themselves? Some of that may be love. But some of that is their response to the strong stream of energy these children have. They are attracting well-being. They are attracting what they need. These children are expressions of well-being.

So, we come to Earth **with** a stream of prosperity. If we are looking outside ourselves for it, we are looking in the wrong place. We already have it coming to us.

For most of us, this is an **Aha!** moment. It was for me.

Well, now the logical question is, if we all come forth with this stream, why do some people have prosperity and others don't?

Because, Hermaden said, *it is then up to you what you do with this stream.*

Will you allow it, or will you resist it?

Will you allow it to flow, or will you pinch it off?

Imagine a spring of water that flows from underground to the top of the earth's surface. Sometimes, the spring flows into a stream or another body of water that provides sustenance to living beings. Other times, humans pinch the flow off. For whatever reason, they choose to resist the flow of water. Sometimes, people think there is a shortage of water, when they are standing on top of an underground spring just feet beneath them. The spring is flowing under the surface of the ground where the humans are standing, but they are focused instead on the dry ground where their feet are planted.

You think you are far away from water, but you are not.

You think you are far away from prosperity, but you are not.

So the first thing you need to understand, Hermaden says, *is that prosperity is already flowing to you.*

But...we may not be allowing it to flow through us, through our energetic and physical bodies, and extending outward into our lives.

We may be keeping it below the surface.

How do we keep it from us?

When the stream of prosperity enters us, and for this purpose imagine it entering through the top of our heads, then it runs immediately into the field of energy that our minds are creating.

Sometimes, mind fields are mine fields.

(The rest of this book is written directly from Hermaden to you.)

What do you believe about prosperity?

Your beliefs about prosperity matter a lot.

This is why, so often, the rich seem to get richer and the poor seem to get poorer. The rich believe they are prosperous and expect the flow to continue. They expect money, or whatever they need, to be there in their lives.

The poor worry about shortage, and worry about not having enough. And therefore don't have enough. They don't expect the money to be there. They worry that it will not flow to them, and therefore they squelch that flow.

These statements are generalizations, and of course won't appear to apply to everyone. **But what is your expectation of money in your life?**

Of course, abundance is about more than money. But for this chapter, we will focus deliberately on money since that is what most of you are asking about.

Your life is a reflection of your expectations.

If you are not sure what you are expecting, just look at your life. It is a manifestation of those expectations.

The stream of prosperity is already flowing to you.

But do your *expectations* allow it to continue to flow?

Do your *thoughts* allow it to continue to flow? Does your thinking impede the flow or enhance the flow?

Where do you direct your focus in your life?

Many people who are wealthy direct much of their attention to the creation and flow of money.

Many people who are poor direct much of their attention to the shortage of money: to bills, to loans, to debt; to figuring out how to overcome a shortage. Or how to stretch out what feels like very little already.

Think about what percentage of your life you spend focused on the allowing of money, and the creation of more money.

We are not talking about attention you pay toward your job, especially if you don't like your job.

How much attention do you pay to the creation of abundance?

Not on creating "enough." Far too many of you spend most of your time on just "enough."

But on really allowing the easy and free flow of money in your lives?

We don't want you to spend a lot of time on this topic right now. But we do want you to spend enough time that you get a realistic sense of where you are directing your attention.

The Universe, and all of us in the non-physical realm, are full of ideas about how you can create more money in your lives – of how you can attract more of what you need and want. Sometimes, there are ways to bring you what you need/want other than money. Abundance is not limited to money. If you think it is, you are squelching your flow.

From the non-physical dimension, we are "feeding" you this information, and these ideas, all the time.

Some people "hear" them and receive the inspiration. And then follow it.

Others do not.

It is not that inspiration is only being offered to some. It is being offered to **all of you, all of the time**.

But not all of you are letting it in.

Sometimes, it is due to a vibrational mismatch. You are not at a frequency that is allowing this information through.

But other times, you do not expect your luck to change. You do not expect wealth, in any form, to come to you. You expect the Universe to deliver only shortage.

Or you receive the ideas and get in your own way, preventing them from manifesting.

Have you ever heard a telephone ring…and ring…and ring, and wondered why no one answered it?

That is the way we often feel.

We are calling, but you aren't answering. You aren't picking up the phone and listening.

Sometimes, you are so busy complaining about where you are and how hard life is that you simply don't allow it to improve.

We can't give you an answer if you aren't listening.

So we invite you to listen.

How will you hear us?

You will hear us, usually, from the inside.

You may have an idea simply come to you.

You may have a feeling that guides you toward something. Because we see the big picture, we are offering you guidance toward what you want, away from what you don't want.

You may "hear" it from a stranger. Or a friend. Or a loved one. If we can't get the thought to you, we will try to get someone else in a more receptive place to share the ideas with you.

The listening, and taking action based on the listening, is still up to you.

Sometimes, some of you are so logical with your resistance that you literally talk yourself out of inspiration. We guide you toward the first step on your path. But you don't see how that path is going to benefit you because you can't see the big picture. We guide you toward the first step, but we know there are a dozen or fifty or five hundred steps on that path. Because you don't see the final step, you don't take the first step.

This is where trust comes in. And faith. And believing in your own knowing, your own internal wisdom.

Think about situations where someone creates something that is, in your culture, a "big invention."

Sometimes, they start with an idea of what they want, and they try to figure out how to make it work.

Sometimes, they start with one piece of the puzzle, and then find a second piece, a third piece. Their invention will keep growing.

Sometimes, they start moving toward Point C, only to find that Point B leads them in a very different direction.

How many of your great inventions have seemingly been accidents? Quite a few.

How many inventors and entrepreneurs benefited from failures along the way? Almost all of them.

Very seldom did everything unfold exactly the way they thought it would.

Or the way they wanted it to.

So, in summary:

There is a stream of prosperity flowing to you. Now.

You are allowing that flow, or pinching it off.

You are allowing inspiration and guidance to what you want.
Or not.

The good news is that you have control over this entire process.

So if you aren't allowing the flow right now, you can.

If you aren't receiving the inspiration we are sending, you can.

If you are receiving the inspiration but not acting on it, you can change that.

If you are focusing more energy on creating shortage than abundance, you can change that too.

You have the power to create more flow.

You have the power to allow more flow.

It is all up to you.

You are not alone in this, because we are here for you. We are here with you.

But you have to be willing to change to allow greater abundance in.

And you can!

You have the power to start, even in this moment, today.

You can do it!

Chapter 3: My Feelings Toward Money

Sometimes, when we talk about having prosperity and abundance, people think we are talking about an abundance of THINGS. And while there is nothing wrong with having an abundance of things, some people seek a multitude of things in an attempt to replace something else in their lives that seems missing – perhaps meaning and purpose, or joy, or loving relationships with others, or a sense of self-worth.

When we talk about prosperity, we are talking about a state of freedom and opportunity. You have the resources – such as time and well-being – to really enjoy your life. You have the means to do what you desire. You enjoy the freedom to do what is fulfilling to you. You have an abundance of desirable choices.

You have an abundance of value in your life. You are creating your life, your own life – a life that is reflective of who you really are, and what matters to you. It is not about satisfying others, but living a life in alignment with your own beliefs.

Human beings are all about expansion. Abundance is a part of that expansion. Prosperity is a part of that expansion. If you had a scrumptious meal today, you would not stop eating for the rest of your life. That would not satisfy your need for food, nor your body's need for nourishment. You would still want to eat again tomorrow. And now, knowing that food can be really tasty, you would likely want as many of your future meals as possible to be delicious. If you are going to eat, and you know that food can be delightful – of course it is natural you would want, hope, expect future meals to taste great. You might even set off on a quest to find more and more delectable food.

There is increasing attention today to having experiences that matter more than things. People want to spend more and more of their present moments feeling fully alive and truly enjoying life.

A lack – a feeling of being impoverished – is a very limiting feeling. It can feel confining and produce much duress and anxiety. Severe lack over a period of time can cause people to feel the life force is draining from them. Depression and powerlessness are not uncommon.

Those feelings of lack can be awful precisely because you know – inside – that is not who you really are, or something you came to earth to experience. You know life should be good for you.

There is nothing wrong with an abundance of things – if that is what you want, and that is meaningful to you. And there is nothing wrong with choosing to have as few things as possible – if that is what you want, and that is meaningful to you.

You get to choose your life. We write about abundance and prosperity because so many people have been disallowing their natural well-being. And we want you to allow it. We want you to allow well-being to flow to you. You deserve it. You are worthy of it. You may have unlearned allowing it, but you can re-learn it with some thoughtful practice. Freedom and well-being are at the core of you.

Let's examine your attitude toward financial abundance. How do you feel about money? Do you believe, like the Biblical saying, that "it is easier for a camel to pass through the eye of a needle than for a rich man to enter the kingdom of heaven?"

Do you believe there is something wrong with having money?

Do you believe you have to work really hard for every dollar, or is it okay for dollars to flow easily to you?

Do you believe your monetary worth is an indicator of your overall worthiness as a human being?

What kinds of beliefs about money did the people have who were around you when you were growing up? How many of those soaked in, and you still believe today?

You don't need to consider these questions in detail. But think about the adults you were around when you were growing up. Did they experience shortage or abundance? Did they *expect* shortage or abundance?

What did you learn from them about money that you still believe to be true today?

As a child, did you believe that money was around you all the time, and you could easily access what you needed? Wanted? Or did you believe that it was hard to get money? That it was elusive?

How many parents teach their children they cannot have what they want because it costs too much and the parents can't afford it?

(We would rather parents teach their children that there are many paths to what they want, and parents are only one of those avenues. If parents can't or choose not to provide something, they can encourage the children to create other channels to what they want. It can be amazing what the Universe will bring when you believe it and allow it.)

We also want you to understand that there is rarely a single route to what you want.

Many people have beliefs that they don't have the education or the skills or the diploma/certificate/license that will allow them to attract sufficient income. Or they believe they are not living in the right place, or they don't know the right people, or they have a handicap of some kind to achieve what they want. None of that has to be true...unless your belief it is true has created that reality for you.

There are people living today with what many of you would consider extreme physical or mental challenges, yet they make an abundant living.

Whatever you see as the handicap or obstacle in your life, don't let it define you. Don't let your past define your future. Don't let past hardship mean future hardship. A past or even current lack of abundance does not mean future lack.

You can change it.

Write down the beliefs you have that are standing in your way of achieving what you want.

Then work your way from each belief to a better feeling place, to a better thinking place.

Work yourself from *can't* to *can*, from *didn't have* to *could have*, from *unworthiness* to *worthiness*.

We have included the tool of *thought steps* later in this book to help you. If you can't get there alone, then try *thought steps* as a way to change your thinking.

Here is what we know.

If you have been experiencing lack, then your beliefs are offering a vibration of lack. If you don't change your beliefs, you cannot change your reality.

If you believe there is a situation in your past, or your present, where you were not treated fairly, then you will continue to experience situations where you feel "it isn't fair."

If you believe you are always somehow at a disadvantage to other people, then you will continue to be.

If you believe you have more challenges in life than most people, then you will continue to have them.

If you believe you have to work hard for every dollar, you will have to continue to work hard.

If you believe rich people are not deserving of their wealth, then you are keeping yourself from ever approaching that category.

If you see wealthy people as "other" and feel they are separate and distinct from you, then you cannot achieve wealth.

(Most of you know people who are financially wealthy, and you probably like them...but you may not know these individuals are wealthy. Most wealthy people do not look or act like the stereotypes in your culture.)

How do you feel about paying taxes? If you resent paying taxes, then you are a vibrational match to an income level that does not pay much in taxes.

True, many wealthy people find ways to channel funds to non-profit agencies and into other avenues so they do not pay much in taxes. But many wealthy people also believe that with much abundance comes much responsibility, and it is important to give back to your community and your government.

There are actually many government services you do emotionally and intellectually support, and would not want to live without. The most obvious are your fire and police services. If you have an emergency, you want help to be available. You have just stopped realizing the connection between the services you do want and your taxes. Most of you believe strongly in public education, and you want the National Guard to be able to respond in a crisis. These are paid for by tax dollars. You want good roads to drive on. And public transportation. These are all physical manifestations of taxes. Most of these are services you are grateful that your society has. So be glad for what tax dollars can provide, and ignore what you don't like. Come into alignment with paying taxes and visualize your dollars flowing into the services you do support.

Do you really want a dislike of taxes to inhibit your ability to increase your wealth?

Did you realize that, for many wealthy people, increasing their income becomes something fun…more like a game?

They like to strategize how to get more interest and earnings on their investments.

They like to play with their money.

Now, that may not be how they see it. They might say they are trying to maximize their income or investment potential. But they enjoy it when they make more money, and don't like it when they make less. Many of them have reached a point of security where they know how much money they have to play with, and how much they need to keep secure to feel safe.

When is the last time you looked at money as something to play with?

As children, you might have played with your food. Maybe you still do.

But when is the last time you played with money?

We are not talking about feeling a shortage, and taking money you need to pay bills, and instead gambling with a desperate hope of winning. We are talking about taking money and playing in a strategy to grow it.

Gambling is gambling. Some people gamble for fun. But people experiencing a shortage seldom gamble just for the fun of it. They gamble from need, from desperation.

Observe who is winning at a casino. It is much more often the people who are having a good time, and less often the people who seem troubled.

(And it is almost always the casinos who are winning by your presence. That is the only guaranteed win.)

Go to a casino for fun. Not because you need money. Buy lottery tickets for fun. Not as an investment in your future.

We aren't saying you won't win. We are saying that you will win more if you are playing – truly *playing, for fun*, and not because you need the money.

Now, we are not sending you to casinos and we are not sending you to buy lottery tickets. But we want you to think about how you are FEELING when you are playing these games. Because most of you are not feeling playful – like you are truly playing – when you choose to participate in these games. And most of you are not losing money you have decided it is okay to lose.

(Yes, some people do participate in these events only for the entertainment value...but that is a very different vibration than shortage. These individuals are only playing what they know they can afford not to take home.)

Now, having considered this concept of gambling, and what you are feeling when you are gambling – think about how you approach the matter of income in your life.

Are you looking at your job, or whatever brings you income, from a broader perspective? Or are you someone who would say you only work for the money?

People who only work for money, then lose their job, will often have a harder time getting a new one, especially if they believe jobs are hard to find.

You need to find value, personal value, in whatever you do.

And that will take us to our next chapter.

Chapter 4: Living the Feeling

How do you feel about your job?

This question assumes you are not retired, but that your current job is the source of most of your income. If you are retired, you might consider your past job or current volunteer work. Or if you would like another position, full or part-time. And being a full-time homemaker is a full-time job – even if it is not a paid position.

If you do not have a job right now and want one, take a piece of blank paper and draw a line down the center of the page, separating it into two columns.

On one side of the page, write "My Last Job" at the top of the page, and then write down how you **felt** about your last job.

On the other side of the page, write down "My Next Job" and then write down how you **want to feel** about your next job.

If you do not like your current job, do the same thing. Your two column headers would be "My Current Job" and "My Next Job." If you are new to the job market and have not held a job yet, your two headers would be "How I Like to Feel When I Work" and "How I Feel Working at My New Job." Because everyone has done some type of work – going to school, cleaning at home, helping someone or volunteering – before they work at their first paying "job."

Include topics like:

> ➢ How I feel going to work
> ➢ How I feel about the work I do
> ➢ How I feel while I am there
> ➢ How I feel about myself while I am there
> ➢ How I feel about my day as I am coming home

> ➢ How I feel about my boss/supervisor
> ➢ How I feel about my co-workers/colleagues
> ➢ How I feel about my work environment
> ➢ How I feel when I tell others what I do and where I work
> ➢ How I feel about the income I make
> ➢ How I feel about any advantages that come with the job (financial or not – whatever you define as a benefit. For instance, the commute, the clothes you wear...any material or non-material advantage.)

Some people love their jobs but hate their paychecks because they don't think they are paid enough. Some people feel they are paid adequately or even generously for what they do. Some people feel their pay is an indication of the respect they are given or the respect they deserve – or indicates a lack of respect.

What is the connection between your job and your income?

Do you think: I chose a field where I knew I wouldn't make much money, but I am doing work that matters to me?

Do you think: I am only doing this job because I couldn't find a better one, or until I find a better one?

Do you think: I am much smarter than my boss but I am probably going to be stuck in this position forever and never be promoted?

Do you think: I love what I am doing and can't believe I actually get paid to do this work?

Your income likely matches how you feel about your job, and what you expect to be paid there.

So if you don't like your income, then you need to shift your expectation.

That might mean finding a new job. Or a new position with the same employer. Or it might mean finding a new career field entirely.

Many people with a lack of money feel boxed into a particular job or field.

We would like you to think about going to a job buffet.

If you could go to a buffet with many wonderful things to do, what would you choose?

Don't think right now about what it would pay you. Just think: what would I do if I got to choose any job? Any career?

You need to step out of your box, if you are in one.

Look around at all the jobs in the world. If you got to pick one, or ten, what would they be?

There is no right or wrong here. Leave monetary compensation out of it. Just think, what work would I like to do?

How would I like to feel about my work?

How would I like to feel about my work environment?

How would I like to feel about the people I work with?

What kind of respect would I like to have?

What kind of autonomy would I like to have?

Start exploring what you would like. Let yourself have choices.

Imagine yourself at a job buffet, and whatever job you tell the server you want, you know you will get it. You know you can take it and try it and see if you like it.

Just imagine.

Now, you may not like where we are going to take you next.

We want you to think about your current job, or your last one, and figure out how you could identify many of those positive qualities within that position. What have you had in past jobs that you would want in future ones?

It is easier to get where you want to go if you already equate your current or last position with the presence of some of these qualities – instead of the lack of them.

Get that? It is a really important point.

How can you find qualities you like in your current or last job, instead of focusing on what you don't/didn't like?

It is easier to get more of what you want if you can find aspects of what is wanted in your present or past life.

We will use an extreme example here...extreme only to some of you.

Let's say you want the freedom to access the rest room when needed. Now, this is an advantage that many of you just assume in your jobs. But for others, they can't assume that freedom. Some truck drivers have to stay with the truck on their daily route, no matter what. Some factory workers must have temporary workers come to their spot to relieve them, or can only access the rest room on breaks or emergencies. Some people must get permission from their supervisors, like a child in school must ask a teacher. Not everyone can use the rest room when they want.

To some people, this freedom means a great deal. Others roll with it...it is not a big deal one way or another. It is just part of the job.

You all have aspects of your job that matter to you a great deal. And some aspects that may not matter as much.

Focus on what you like, and what you want.

Remember that the law of attraction will bring more to you of where you are directing your attention.

If you resent not having the freedom to use the rest room when you want, then that will likely stay an issue for you in this job...and the next.

You need to make peace with where you are, while – at the same time – deciding it is okay to want more.

So in this situation, you might say, if it is true, "I have adjusted to getting permission. It's not a big deal." At the same time, you might think, "It will be nice when I have a job where I have the freedom to make these choices on my own."

We want you to make peace with where you are. It is fine to ask for more. But it is easier for more to come to you if you are okay with where you are now.

We know that sounds counter-intuitive.

Here is what we are not telling you. We don't want you to settle in your life, not long-term, for less than you want. You might need to settle in the short-term, but then you can work to change your future to be more inclusive of what you want.

You may not like where you are standing right now. But we want you to realize that you are always moving forward, always evolving. You don't have to create more of the same. You can create something new – something better, happier.

We want you to be happy, remember?

But we don't want you to lose the job today you are dependent on to pay your bills.

We don't want you to settle for less than you want, but we don't want you to live in hardship, either.

This is about intention.

From wherever you are right now, think about where you intend to go – where you want to go.

You can't stand where you are, not liking it, and expect to get somewhere better.

The Universe will keep matching your vibration to where you are. It will match you with what is the dominant vibration in your life.

Decide where you want to be. Envision how it will feel. Find evidence of that in your life now. Take inspired action to get there.

These are four separate steps.

1) What do you want?

2) How does it feel to have what you want? If you were living it right now, how would it feel? Make that feeling real.

3) Find the feeling of what you want *as it already exists in your life now.* You might need to take little things and exaggerate them, expand the feeling – but find evidence for what you want in your **now**.

4) The Universe will match you up with what you want, with what you are feeling. It will bring you more situations to match those feelings. Make it real in the present and it will be real in the future.

The non-physical realm will offer you guidance and inspiration toward those next steps, toward what you are asking for. But as we have mentioned earlier, you need to listen. And you need to follow those steps.

Here is what non-physical will not tell you: that you need to quit your day job and struggle financially in order to eventually, finally, live your dreams.

It simply doesn't work that way.

Ask non-physical to show you how you can live more of what you want by still having a solid financial foundation.

If you don't have a solid financial foundation right now, then that is the first question to ask: how do I get there?

There are so many times that someone is guided to a part-time job while looking for full-time employment, and doesn't take it because it is only part-time. But we know that part-time job will eventually lead to what they want. It is on the path to what is wanted. It might be better to work two (or more) part-time jobs where you are really happy at one of them, than to work a full-time job where you are miserable.

Think about how the Universe is reading it.

If you are happy twenty hours a week, that is twenty hours where you are vibrating well-being and the Universe is bringing you more of that. If you are miserable forty hours a week, then the Universe is bringing you twice as much misery.

A happy part-time job can be on the path to a happy full-time job.

Chapter 5: Initiator or Responder?

Are you an initiator or a responder?

Many people live their lives by responding to their circumstances and to the people around them. They let others set the emotional frequency in conversations. They stay in jobs they don't like because at least they know the circumstances of that job. The same goes for relationships. They feel like they "put up" with what is in their lives. They are making the best of the cards they feel life has dealt them. They aren't trying to change their lives. They may not be happy, but they assume that's the way life is. You resign yourself to live or work where you are. Or some resign themselves and then complain about it to others, yet have no intention of changing it.

Other people take the initiative for what is going on in their lives. If they don't like something, they change it. They make something better.

Imagine using a recipe in the kitchen to make some cookies. There is an ingredient you don't like. But the recipe calls for it, so you put it in anyway. Then you complain about the nuts or raisins or coconut in the cookies.

Baker #1 just responds to the recipe.

But now imagine having a recipe that you want to make, but you clearly don't like one of the ingredients. So you decide to improvise. You will leave it out, or make a substitution. If you don't like the finished cookies, you consider what you would do differently next time. As Baker #2, you recognize your role in creating the cookies.

In truth, both of these bakers are creating their lives, and co-creating with the Universe.

But Baker #2 is doing it recognizing personal power. Baker #1 is feeling a lack of power, and demonstrating that.

Most people have times in their lives they initiate, and times they respond. You are not 100% one way. You are a mix.

When someone is considered charismatic, that person usually sets the tone, the frequency, with his or her presence.

If happy, the room feels happy while this person is there.

If unhappy, the room also feels that.

A charismatic person does not allow others to set the tone, the feeling. He or she brings a strong sense of energy to the situation.

It feels great to be around charismatic people who feel good. Because everyone in their presence will feel brighter and happier too.

When people assume responsibility for their own happiness, they carry their happiness with them.

Do you feel empowered to create your own happiness?

No one can take that power from you, or keep it from you.

You have the ability to create a happy life.

You are the only one who can create a happy life for yourself.

Are you doing it?

Chapter 6: Thinking Thoughts that Serve Me

You are responsible for your own happiness.

The next logical statement might appear to be: you are responsible for your own financial ease.

But here is where the problem comes in.

Many of you who are struggling with not-enoughness in your lives are blaming yourselves for that lack.

Your society, for the most part, doesn't blame people who aren't happy. It doesn't say: shame on you for being unhappy. (We are setting aside the shame/blame associated with what society calls "mental illness" which is a different topic entirely.)

But there is a definite sense of blame placed on people living in financial discomfort.

There is often a sense that they are doing something, or did something, wrong.

They didn't get enough education.

They weren't ambitious enough.

They didn't finish something they started.

They didn't assume the responsibility of providing for their family.

They can be seen as irresponsible by society. There is a sense they did something wrong.

What we know, and understand, is that often, **they were simply thinking thoughts that did not serve them.**

Yes, it really is that simple.

There are lots of billionaires who didn't finish school. Displeased their parents. Followed hobbies as careers that their family members considered unproductive. Were even considered lazy by a traditional work ethos. Maybe teachers said they were stupid. Maybe they "just" sat at their computers all day.

But: they were initiators.

They accepted their own personal power.

Either they refused to accept blame, or they were driven by it.

They did not allow it to crush their spirit, or diminish their dreams, or squelch what they thought they could achieve in life.

They went forward anyway.

These are the people who will walk into the woods when there is no clear path, and they will create their own path.

These are the people who will stand and knock at a closed door, instead of walking away from it.

These are the people who are determined to move forward in life.

If you don't like where you are financially, we want you to tell yourself:

I learned to think thoughts that didn't serve me. I am not going to do that anymore. And I am going to let myself off the hook for where I am now.

Where you are now is simply evidence of those thoughts. It is the energetic patterns made manifest in the physical. But it is not representative of who you really are, or what life has in store for you.

You get to determine that.

It doesn't matter how old you are. Or how young you are.

You get to determine that.

If you have been beating yourself up for where you are, stop it.

It does not serve you.

If you spend time around others who beat you up for where you are, stop it.

Spending time with those beliefs does not serve you.

Either tell those individuals to stop sharing their opinions. Or choose other people to spend time with who will recognize your inherent self-worth.

We want you to understand that the people in your life may change, sometimes significantly, as you move from lack of prosperity to abundant prosperity.

You need to accept that a vibrational change from one frequency to another will often affect much that is in your life.

We want you to accept that climbing higher will bring you wonderful new people and experiences.

Getting to a higher frequency financially will often be accompanied by many other changes.

A rising tide lifts all boats.

But a boat that is moored with a very short rope may not be able to rise much.

A higher frequency can affect much that is in your life.

The first change is to stop thinking thoughts that don't serve you, and replace them with thoughts that do.

You cannot just stop thinking certain thoughts.

You need to replace them.

Consider your old, non-beneficial thoughts like an old story.

You need to tell a new story...perhaps many new stories.

And as you find yourself starting to tell an old story, stop yourself. Press the pause button. Ask yourself, do I want to keep telling that story? Do I want to keep living that story? If the story has not served you in the past, then you need to stop telling it/thinking it now, and find a new, better story instead.

What story would you like to be telling about your life? About yourself?

How can you find aspects of those stories to tell now that feel true...that are true?

Think about the future you want to live. What in that future can you find in your present? What in that future can you find in your past?

Take some time to really answer these questions, and write them down.

If you are experiencing shortage now, but have had enough in the past, then you can start to tell yourself: **I know the feeling of enough. I like having enough. It feels good to have enough.** Think about what you do have enough of now.

Even if you are homeless, you can find enough of something you do like in your present experience: I have enough of...grass. Clouds. Open spaces. (Or maybe tall buildings. Cement. People. Windows.)

Even if you are in prison, you can often find enough food or water or cover from the elements. There is likely an abundance of metal and cement.

What do you have enough of?

Where can you find abundance in your life?

Look around today determined to find abundance. You will be surprised at what you find, and where you find it. Things you take for granted every day, you will begin to see.

You are surrounded by abundance. Whether it is grains of sand, blades of grass, clouds or concrete. Everyone has abundance of something in their lives.

Find it. Identify it.

Begin to see yourself as living in a Universe of Abundance. All around you.

You are in the midst of it. It surrounds you.

Abundance is already in your life in many forms.

Chapter 7: General Statements of Well-Being

It is very helpful to have some general statements of positive belief that you carry with you. These need to be default statements that you can bring forward in your thoughts whenever needed. They are like handy tools you keep close and reach for often.

You might bring your statements forward when you are anxious or worried. If you catch yourself thinking or saying something not of benefit to you, reach instead for a general statement of well-being. You can use it as a replacement thought if you catch yourself thinking a resistant thought.

These statements should apply to many situations. That's why they are general!

They must feel true to you: they must resonate with you and with your beliefs.

For instance, you might believe: *Everything is always working out for me*. You may not know how or when. But you have had hard times before, and you always made it through.

The Universe has my back.

I am always loved and supported.

Non-physical guidance is always available to me.

I know I am going to be all right. You don't need the particulars of how it is going to work out. But you have been in struggles before, and always came through on the other side.

My life is getting better and better.

Good things are happening for me.

I will be okay. In fact, I am okay right now, in this moment.

This situation is temporary. Well-being is mine.

Avoid cliché statements that you don't believe. If you are a religious person, you may find a helpful statement in a religious text.

You want your statements to feel true, but also hopeful. You need a statement that will reassure you when you feel stressed.

Sometimes, it can be hard to feel that well-being is dominating our lives. But most people experience more positive, or at least neutral, than negative in their lives. Even during the bleakest of times, we can find positive things if we look for them.

Find a statement that reasserts your well-being, and let it become your new mantra. You may want to try several on for a while, and see which ones bring you the greatest relief and reassurance.

Repeat it to yourself when you are waiting in line at a store, or sitting in traffic. Allow it to become a default thought in how you think about your life, a practiced vibration. Keep this thought active in your life so you can find it easily. Use it often.

Chapter 8: Enjoying the Journey

Some people ask us, why do you write such short chapters?

Each chapter introduces new thoughts, and we want you to recognize that there is a slight vibrational shift happening from chapter to chapter.

We are taking you a step higher. Then another step higher.

We also want you to feel like you are making easy progress in reading this book.

And while some of you will start at the beginning of the book and read through to the end, other readers will skip around. While many chapters build on earlier concepts, we try to make most chapters sufficiently self-contained as to be helpful to the casual reader.

As you work your way through these chapters, we hope you will find yourself starting to feel a little better about where you are. And about where you want to be. And we want you to realize that you have the power to get there – you <u>are</u> getting there.

A step at a time.

We are modeling what we are teaching.

Just take a step at a time.

Don't expect quantum leaps.

Think about how many people win the lottery, only to lose their winnings. Or who say later that winning was a horrible experience.

Not everyone is ready for it vibrationally.

Those who are ready use their winning as a step to live more abundantly, permanently.

Those who are not will not stay in financial abundance.

Think about people who win the lottery...again...and again.

It is actually easier to win a second time than a first time. Because now you have a physical experience that tells you it really is possible. You can do it.

(And while most of you think of the lottery only in terms of the financial gain, there can be much more vibrationally attached to winning than simply the financial prize.)

It is not that some people are simply lucky. But some people believe they are lucky. Some people expect good things to happen to them. They have belief systems that allow for improvement. Hope.

What do you expect in your life?

If you feel you are stuck and can't get out of a rut, then you can't.

Your belief is making it difficult for you.

In truth, you continue to create over and over what you believe.

No one is ever stuck. Time is always moving forward.

You can keep re-creating the same thing.

But it is a re-creation that feels like being stuck, because you believe you aren't making progress.

If you can see that, then you can change it.

To begin shifting the feeling of stuckness, try saying: "I have been re-creating a feeling of stuckness, over and over again.

And now I am going to create a feeling of moving forward, toward what I want."

We would encourage you to think about times you have felt movement after a period of feeling stuck – how good that felt. Get inside that emotion.

If you are in a car in the middle of a traffic jam, even slow movement feels better than being stopped. It always feels better to start moving again. There is relief.

Find the feeling of relief.

What does it feel like for you? When have you felt it before?

Make a list.

Then let yourself experience that feeling again.

Allow it.

Create it.

Recognize it, and give yourself credit for moving forward in your life again.

The journey to greater abundance is just that: a journey. It takes time to get from where you are to where you want to be. But this is a creative process, and you are meant to have fun along the way. Creating more money in your life can be a lot of fun! And can be a very enjoyable process. Enjoying the journey is an important part of the path.

Resistance can be like glare in your eyes when you are driving. It can interfere with your vision, and keep you from seeing the progress you are making. **Your prosperity is**. Being prosperous is natural to you. It is a part of who you are. By looking at what has not <u>yet</u> manifested in your life, you are not seeing what <u>is</u> manifesting. Look for the evidence that prosperity is manifesting. The evidence may be subtle, but it is there. Find it. Congratulate yourself on your progress.

Remember that you are the creator of your experience. This is not about someone else deciding you are worthy. This is not about you finally being deserving enough so prosperity is bestowed upon you. There is no one holding power over you, keeping you from manifesting what you want in your life. You might think there is. But this is not a universe of assertion – no one can keep you from having what you want. Of course, you might think they can. But the law of attraction is about you attracting what you have asked for, what you are a vibrational match to. You alone have the power to align and let it into your experience. No one else does.

Love the journey. Embrace your power. Find your own happiness, and insist every day that you feel good. Be fussy about how you feel. You must be true to your own desires, and align with allowing them into your life. There is no turning back. Once you have expanded – becoming more – you need to align and allow this *expanded you* to have the full life you desire.

Be more optimistic. Find clarity – it's there. Take the leap that the contrast of your past experience with lack has caused energetically. Give your attention to what is going right on this journey, to what feels so very wonderful. Getting to where you want to be can be a lot of fun – and so can the path there. Enjoy!

Chapter 9: Tolerating Not Feeling Good

Not feeling good.

Anytime we talk to people who have not had abundance in their lives for a while, we know there have almost always been other things in their lives about which they have also not been feeling good.

The lack of abundance is an indicator. It is an indicator of not feeling good.

We wish this would resound with you like we were shouting it from a rooftop: **you have come to accept not feeling good. You have learned to tolerate negative emotion. You have become much too tolerant of negative emotion.**

When you learned to adjust yourself to not feeling good about one thing, you learned to adjust to not feeling good about other things.

Let's give you an example.

Let's say there is a beautiful, wonderful child who worries about something. Her parents have taught her about worry. It is pretty common for people in her family to worry. So she learns to worry.

Worry is not a good feeling. But this child gets pretty good at it.

Eventually, this child worries about all sorts of things, just like the grownups around her.

Maybe she worries about having enough to eat. Or the grownups having too little money. Maybe she worries about being too fat or too thin, too tall or too short, too pretty or not pretty enough. Maybe she worries about being too smart or not smart enough, being lonely or being popular. Maybe she worries about not being enough – whatever that is to her – or not having enough. Maybe she worries about not feeling good, or the grownups around her not feeling good. She learns to worry, and accept worry as a part of life. That is what one does, she thinks: if one is alive, one worries.

Worry is a part of her life. She has grown accustomed to it. She is still a child, but she is a child who worries.

Now, we think you would all agree that being worried means you are not feeling good. You cannot be happy and be worried at the same time. The vibrations are too far apart.

So today, if we asked you: you can choose to be worried or you can choose to be happy. Which would you choose?

This child chose worry because it was the frequency of many adults around her. She knew it did not feel good to worry. But the grownups around her made it seem normal – a normal part of life.

When she was very young, she didn't tolerate feeling negative emotion. As a baby, when she didn't feel good she would cry. She knew, inherently, she should feel good.

But the grownups around her felt negative emotion a lot, and put up with it. They gradually taught her to put up with it too. So she learned to not feel good. She actually spent a lot of time not feeling good.

The ache in her stomach told her that worry was not good for her. The anxiety she felt told her that too. So did the nightmares she sometimes had.

Her emotions told her first that worry was not good for her. But she learned to overrule her feelings – the grownups taught her concepts like "controlling" her emotions. She had to learn to control her anxiety, control her worry – like they did. That's what they told her.

So, over time, as she continued to not listen to her internal guidance that worry was not healthy for her, and instead listened to guidance coming from humans who thought worry was a part of earthly life – she developed some physical symptoms. Her emotions told her first, because worry felt bad. *Worry is not good for you. Worry separates you from Source. Source is not worried.* Over time, her body tried to get her attention, to stop worrying. But she didn't listen to that either, just like the grownups around her didn't listen to their guidance.

Now she started having physical symptoms more often. So the adults started worrying about her, and took her to doctors, who also worried about her. And she started to worry about her body, and going to doctors, and taking tests, and now she and all the grownups believed there was something wrong with her.

A "good" day now for her was a day she did not have a stomach ache or a nightmare, a day when she didn't bite her nails or feel sick with worry. It wasn't about having days anymore when she actually felt good. It was now about having days when she didn't feel as bad.

Many of you will relate to this situation in some way. Your lives may not fit this example perfectly. But you can think about things in your life you weren't feeling good about, and you gradually came to accept not feeling good as normal. Feeling less than good on a regular basis became acceptable.

And what we want you to understand is that this pattern – of *feeling*, of *thought*, of accepting *less than* – gradually had a huge effect on your vibrational offering. You became tolerant of not feeling good.

And what started for our beautiful child as worry then expanded to other things in her life as she grew older. So in addition to the things she worried about as a child, the older she got, the more she found to worry about.

Remember that the Universe assumes you give something your attention on purpose. If you give it your attention, you are doing it by choice. Which means you like it and want more of it. The Universe does not make judgments or evaluations about where you direct your attention. It does not sift out topics according to what you want or don't want. If you are giving it your attention, you must like giving it your attention.

So if you feel worry toward one thing, the Universe will gradually bring you a second thing to worry about. And a third. And so on. Because the more you are worrying – or feeling whatever negative emotion is in your life – the more the Universe is going to bring you things that will evoke that same emotion from you.

If, like this child, you have come to accept not feeling good as a normal part of your life, then the Universe will bring you more to feel that way about.

And because you have learned to tolerate not feeling good, you won't immediately throw a fit and change the condition causing the problem.

Young children throw tantrums when they don't feel good. They know they are supposed to feel good. And if they don't, then they are going to scream and throw a fit until the world fixes itself and they feel better.

But over time, the grownups teach the children to tolerate not feeling good. So they stop crying. They stop throwing tantrums.

You, too, learned to tolerate negative conditions in your life. And as you did, the vibration became more entrenched in your life. So that when you want to change one of these conditions, like lack of abundance, you feel like you are swimming upstream. It feels really hard to do. Because you have been swimming against the flow of well-being for a long time. You have been swimming against good-feeling things in your life. You have been swimming against well-being and positive emotions.

So now, when you are trying to improve your abundance, you are dealing with vibrational patterns that have been around a long time. It is like laying down train tracks that you have been traveling – in some cases, for many years. And now you want to lay new train tracks. And you are finding it really hard to do. Because you have been going over those old tracks for so long that it seems like the natural thing to do.

We want you to understand it is the practiced thing you have been doing, but not the natural thing to do.

The natural thing for you to do has always been *to feel good*. To have abundance. To enjoy well-being. To know yourself as an extension of Divine Source Energy. To know your worthiness so thoroughly that there is no doubt your life should unfold joyously, easily, you should have what you want. YOU SHOULD FEEL GOOD. YOU SHOULD BE HAPPY.

Most of you have forgotten this. Most of you have accepted not feeling good for a long time. Perhaps about one thing in your life; perhaps about many. And now you want to feel better. We want you to feel better. We have always wanted you to be happy and have what you want. We want you to feel loved and know your worth. We want you to know your power. We want you to live in love and joy and enjoy a life that is fulfilling. We want you to *CLAIM IT NOW!*

But...what does that mean?

First, it means you stop tolerating negative emotion in your life. You insist on living a joyful life, and on having thoughts that feel good.

Second, it means you have to lay new tracks. You have to be intentional in feeling good and laying new tracks in your life that create new patterns, new habits, that embrace feeling good.

Let's imagine that you wrap a string around your wrist every time you engage in a particular habit. Pretend you engage in this pattern of thought – for instance, worrying – every single day. If you just did it one day, then it would be easy to break the string – easy to break the habit. But if you did it many days, even years, you would have many strings to break, and that would seem harder.

The good news is that you don't have to pull all the old strings off your wrist. You just need to stop adding new strings. You need to begin a new habit.

Which means...you need to be kind to yourself, gentle to yourself, as you start to lay new tracks. You need to realize that you have been on these rails for a long time, and it will take some time to lay new tracks and adjust to life on the new tracks.

So...don't be hard on yourself. Sometimes you will find yourself on the old tracks simply out of habit.

When you do that, just catch yourself and get back on the new tracks. Don't beat yourself up. Don't condemn yourself. Just laugh and say, "Look where I am – old tracks! I'm moving back to the new tracks now."

We also want you to understand that *you have to lay new tracks*. You can't just get off the old tracks. Your train – your mind – must have new tracks to get onto.

For instance, you can't tell yourself, "Don't think that." You need a replacement thought. You need to switch to where you want to go.

Your train won't move anywhere new unless you lay new tracks. So you have to lay new tracks before you stop going over the old tracks again and again.

What do we mean by new tracks?

Chapter 10: Laying New Thoughts

Imagine that you have a model railroad, or maybe you prefer a toy train, running somewhere in your home. You have laid out a pattern of tracks for this train to ride across. If you did not lay out tracks with forethought, and the pieces did not connect or the curves were too sharp, the train would derail and crash. So you have carefully laid out the design, thinking just how and where you want this train to run.

Most of you have developed patterns of thought like these train tracks. Except many of you set up your initial train tracks without a lot of planning and forethought. You did not consider: where do I want to direct my attention? How do I want my train – my mind – to run? And where? How do I want to feel while I ride these tracks?

Most of you set up these pieces of track according to what you learned from the grownups close to you when you were young, adding this piece from your parents/caregivers, that piece from your teachers, and this piece from coaches or other adults. This piece of track you got from other kids in your life.

There was not an overall plan that you set forth before starting. You learned these things from the adults around you in the process of growing up. You added one piece at a time over many years.

Now we are asking you, which thoughts serve you, and which do not?

We are inviting you to lay a new set of tracks intentionally. You can plan it. Decide what you want. Decide what tracks will serve you and which won't; which thoughts will serve you and which won't.

We are inviting you to lay new tracks according to where you want your life to go, how you want your life to be. Choose which thoughts feel good. Look at each piece of track before you lay it, and ask yourself if it feels right and if it will help get you where you want to go.

You all know where you want to go. Even if you don't know the specifics of where you want to go, you know the general aspects. You know how you want to feel, for instance. Which feelings matter to you the most, and which feelings do you want to have in your life? Which thoughts will help you to have those feelings more?

If you were literally setting up a train track in your home, you would think first about where you want it to go. Maybe you set it up in one room and then decide to move it elsewhere. But you give it deliberate thought. You think about the space you need, where you will see it best, what layout will satisfy your objectives. You plan ahead. You lay it out with intention.

That is what we are asking you to do. Think about what you want in your life, how you want your life to feel, and then what thoughts will best satisfy your intentions.

You have this amazing emotional guidance system that will help you do that. Thoughts that move you toward what you want will feel good to you. Thoughts that move you away from what you want will not feel good.

So, let's say you want to have a thought of being worthy: *I am a worthy being.* That should feel good to you. If you instead think, "I am not a worthy being," you would not feel good.

The best thoughts will resonate with the Source within you, and feel great.

If you have a thought that you are worthier than someone else, that will not feel as good. Because Source knows you are both worthy. Trying to compare yourself to someone else does not serve you.

If you have a thought, *I am greatly loved*, that thought serves you – and is true.

If you have a thought, "I am not loved as much as I want to be" – that does not serve you. And is not true. You are all loved tremendously from non-physical, and if you don't feel that, then you are simply separating yourself from that love. It does not mean you are not loved – you are just not allowing yourself to tune to the love coming from us.

Now, everyone's tracks will be laid out differently. We are not going to tell you what to think, because we can't. What you think is your own business. But we are going to urge you to choose your thoughts intentionally, thinking about what feels good to you.

Model train tracks are designed according to gauges. But tracks within the same gauge can be interchangeable. So this is not a one-time activity, to set up the layout of your train tracks. Over time, as your frequency raises, you will have better feeling thoughts that you can switch to. So a thought might feel good to you now, and you incorporate it into your design. Then a few weeks or months or years later, you have a better feeling thought and you replace it.

So think in terms of *now*. You are laying out the tracks that feel good to you *now*. But this is not a permanent design, because you are an expanding, evolving being. Your thoughts will continue to shift, continue to change over time. So don't worry about this being a permanent layout because it will continue to evolve as you do.

Doesn't that thought alone feel better to you? You don't have to create the perfect layout of tracks for all time – you couldn't! You just need to find thoughts that feel good to you **now**.

It is important to remember that it is not the thoughts themselves, but their vibrational offering that really matters. It is not just what you think, but how you feel as you think it.

If you think, *I am a worthy being*, and that feels good to you, then that thought works for you. Include it in your tracks.

But if you think, *I am a worthy being*, and a part of you inside responds something like "no way" or "that's a joke," then you do not want to lay that thought in your tracks. Because you are also laying those emotions with it, and those emotions will not move you into a positive place in your life.

Think of some positive statements and see how they resonate with you. Here are some examples:

I am a lovable being.

I am a loving being.

I embrace well-being in my life.

I know all is well.

Everything is always working out for me.

The Universe is always taking really good care of me.

I am taking really good care of me.

I am a successful being.

I am enjoying great success in my life.

I am enjoying success now.

I am surrounding myself with people who are supportive of what I want to do with my life.

I am surrounding myself with people I really enjoy.

I put nutritious, nourishing food and drink into my body.

I love moving and celebrating the physicality of this life.

I am enjoying this journey in life. I am enjoying MY journey in life.

I am having more and more fun all the time.

The path to what I want is unfolding easily. It is lighting up one step at a time.

I can feel Source calling me to what I want. I am listening and coming – coming home to what I want.

Chapter 11: Feeling Economic Hindrance

What does it mean to feel economically hindered? It means that there is something you really want, but feel you can't have or do because you don't have enough money. It is one thing to want something, not have enough money, but decide to save for it so you can purchase it in the future. That is not a feeling of being hindered, but of being in the process of affording it. Maybe you are in the process of affording a house or car or vacation. Maybe you are in the process of affording something much smaller. But you are actively saving for it, or planning how to earn the money or otherwise tap the resources that will allow you to have what you want.

Think about a child who really, really wants something and is saving for it, perhaps doing things to earn money toward fulfilling this desire. This child does not feel hindered. The child knows that he/she is capable of having this thing, and is in the process of acquiring the resources to buy it.

Feeling fully in a state of being economically hindered is something that happens over a period of time. There is something you want you cannot afford. Then another thing. And another thing. Over time, you start to feel really hindered by your lack of ability to create the resources to secure what you desire/need.

This feeling could be for small things or big things. You might feel hindered from buying the food you want to eat. Or you might feel hindered from traveling the way you would like.

If this feeling starts to affect the way you perceive the world, then it can become contagious in your life. You can't afford one thing, then another, then another. If you stay focused on feeling economically hindered long enough, the Universe will respond to your feeling this way by bringing you more things to evoke and match that feeling.

Feeling economically hindered long enough can eventually result in you feeling hindered in other ways in your life. The feeling of hindered can spread. Maybe you start to develop manifestations in your body and feel physically hindered. Maybe you start to feel hindered in skills you need to work or to fully enjoy a hobby. Maybe you feel hindered in relationships, or by a relationship.

If this feeling of being economically hindered resonates with you, then ask yourself if there are other areas of your life where you are feeling hindered?

Have you been feeling hindered for a long time?

It does not matter how long, or how many areas of your life. But if this is part of a pattern in your life, then it just lets you know you have some momentum going on this topic. And it may take a little while to create the change you would like. So be patient with yourself.

Sometimes, we have laid tracks with beliefs we didn't even realize we had.

But if you have identified this, then it is time to lay new tracks.

The first part is to see if you are feeling hindered generally, or if you are feeling hindered by someone or something. Sometimes, people feel hindered by something without blaming someone for it. For instance, maybe Person A feels hindered by weighing too much, but assumes responsibility for it. But Person B feels hindered by weight, and blames his parents. He feels hindered, but he doesn't assume responsibility for the hindrance and he feels a change is beyond his control. He sees it as someone else's fault.

Maybe someone else feels hindered by caring for parents or children or a spouse, or by responsibilities at work or home that don't feel fair. There can be many reasons to feel hindered.

But what you do with that feeling is important.

Do you feel that you have control – or even influence – over the source or manifestation of that hindrance?

For instance, a child who grows into an adult feeling unloved and unwanted, and feels like she was a hindrance to her parents and kept them from living the lives they wanted to live...may have issues with self-esteem. If she starts to feel like a burden, then she will enter into other relationships that bring her more evidence of that – that she is a burden. Eventually she may develop physical manifestations that support her strong feeling that she is a burden. Even if the people around her didn't view her initially as a burden, they may eventually come to see her that way because it is her strong belief that she is a burden.

It doesn't matter if she was not a burden if she felt like one. If she feels like a burden, the Universe will eventually yield her evidence to prove (to her) that she is a burden. And eventually the others in her life will likely yield to this very strong belief she is emanating, and start to feel as she does: she is a burden.

If you feel hindered for a long time, in any area of your life, you will probably start to see other manifestations in your life of that feeling.

Likewise, if you feel angry or frustrated that you have not been treated fairly, you will see other evidence of that develop.

Part of what is helpful to realize is that the Universe is not out to get you, to hinder you, to treat you unfairly. It is simply responding to what you are offering vibrationally.

Didn't get that job and think you should have? Think the candidate who got the job wasn't as qualified? Feel you are being discriminated against in some way?

The way you are being treated is a result of your beliefs.

Change your beliefs, and you will see miracles occur.

But realize that you are the Source of these manifestations: your beliefs. Because the Universe will always yield evidence to you that what you believe is true.

That is one of the ironic jokes about law of attraction. If someone doesn't believe in the law of attraction, then the law of attraction will bring him evidence to confirm what he believes. The law of attraction will support his belief that the law doesn't exist.

Haven't you seen evidence of that with someone in your life?

You can't change someone else's vibrational offering.

And they can't change yours.

If you want to observe someone who is successful and learn how their beliefs function in the world, spend some time with them. See if they will let you go to work with them for a day, just to observe. Read books they recommend or have written. Watch videos they like or have made. If they are being authentic, then you will begin to see their beliefs emerge – and their vibrational patterning. Ask the Universe to help show you how and what they are thinking, how and what they believe. They are modeling success. They are modeling, for you, how to think and emanate vibrational success.

They can model for you a different world view. If it feels right to you, consider trying it on...like you might try a new shirt you wouldn't usually wear. Try on a mindset, as an experiment, and play with it. See how the world responds to you.

You need to open your mind, and your expectations, to different results. If you don't expect it to work, then of course, it can't. But play with new thoughts, new beliefs, new tracks. See how the Universe responds.

Chapter 12: Fairness

Another belief which often holds people back from allowing financial prosperity is the sense that: it's not fair.

It doesn't have to be a belief about financial prosperity but often a feeling of unfairness encompasses it.

Is there something in your life you believe isn't fair? Wasn't fair?

And if that is true, if that resonates with you, then see if there are other areas of your life where you have also been practicing that belief.

Some examples:

...If you believe you aren't paid enough, or someone else received a promotion you should have.

...If you believe you are burdened with caring for someone, while you believe another person should be providing more care, sharing more evenly.

...If you believe you didn't receive a fair settlement from a divorce, lawsuit, will.

...If you share child care, or child care expenses, and believe there is an imbalance.

...If you work harder than your colleagues, but receive the same (or less) pay.

...If your life partner earns more money than you, but works less.

...If you invested in a stock which lost money, but you believe shouldn't have.

...If you believe you have something holding you back, despite your capabilities.

...If you find unfairness in politics, local or world events.

Unfairness is not just a thought or belief: it is a feeling.

And it is a powerful feeling!

If you feel something in your life is unfair, there is usually strong feeling accompanying it.

And when there is strong feeling, there is strong attraction.

So where you start feeling unfair about one thing, you eventually end up feeling many things in your life are not fair. Because feeling strongly about one thing attracts another situation you will feel is unfair. And another. And another.

Even if you didn't start off feeling there was something unfair about your financial situation, soon enough you will have attracted enough unfairness into your life that it may well end up affecting your financial situation.

Consider your parents, or the place where you grew up.

Was there a sense of fairness there, or a sense of unfairness?

Was there a sense of financial fairness or financial unfairness?

Sibling rivalry suggests unfairness. Parental favoritism suggests unfairness.

A divorce or separation can be interpreted by one party (or both) as unfair.

If there was not enough money, or there were not enough jobs, the adults may have felt unfairness.

And if they did, while you were growing up, you may have picked up a sense from those adults that the world is not fair...or not fair to you, or your family.

This is not a blame game, where you want to blame someone else for your beliefs.

This is just about awareness: do you have these beliefs today? Are they affecting your life?

Beliefs of unfairness can manifest feelings under many different labels, including resentment, jealousy, anger, frustration, envy, blame, vengefulness or hatred, to name just a few.

If you spend a lot of time in your life feeling one of these other strong negative emotions, see if there is a thread of unfairness somewhere in your thinking.

Spend some time over the next few days focusing on FAIRNESS.

See if the people around you comment on fairness or unfairness...if they have feelings one way or the other. (They may not.)

See if you find yourself judging situations as fair or unfair.

Then start *looking for fair*: realizing that everything that people are living is a match to what they are vibrationally offering.

The reality with the law of attraction is that you are attracting, and living, a life that represents your beliefs and emotions.

You can't live "fair" if you view the world as unfair.

You can't energetically allow prosperity into your life if that would rebalance the scales in your favor, or even equally...and you believe you have been, or are being, treated unfairly.

You need to let "unfair" go.

As challenging as it may be to understand, from a law of attraction perspective, there is no unfairness in this world.

Everything everyone is living is a perfect vibrational match to the vibration they are emanating, to what they believe and feel.

If you want fairness, you need to understand that. And yes, embrace that.

That doesn't mean not feeling sympathy for people who have not figured that out yet, who are not creating their lives intentionally.

But it does mean you need to accept that any past or present unfairness in your life is the result of your energetic field. And thus, you participated – vibrationally – in co-creating it.

You may not like it.

But life is fair – vibrationally.

Wealth is fair.

Blaming others for your misfortune will not bring you greater fortune. Accept that your life is simply a reflection of your vibrational emanation to the world.

Then accept responsibility for your own wealth.

And start creating a greater flow: start allowing the prosperity **that is yours!**

Chapter 13: Luck

Do you consider yourself to be lucky?

People often think of themselves as lucky or unlucky. A winner or not.

Would you say that life goes your way most of the time?

That when you want something, you get it?

That you are a fortunate person?

Now, we know many of you answered, "I create my own luck."

Because if you understand you create your own life through the energetic field you offer, then you also understand that you create your own luck—or lack of it.

But what do you believe about yourself and your own good luck...your own good fortune?

Let's say you have just finished a meal where you were given a plate of fortune cookies.

Some people expect to have a very fortunate saying inside their cookies.

Some don't care.

Some hesitate and worry a bit if the fortune is not positive, like it might be a premonition.

(After all, they are called fortune cookies – not misfortune cookies.)

We can apply this situation to many experiences in your life.

When you buy a lottery ticket, do you expect it to win?

When you enter a contest, do you expect a prize? Or do you just enter for the fun of it?

When you apply for a job you really want, do you expect to be called for an interview?

When you invite someone to go somewhere with you, do you consider it likely they will join you?

When you pull your vehicle into a busy parking lot, do you expect to easily find a parking place?

What are your expectations about good fortune in your life?

We would like ALL of you to think:

I am a very lucky person.

Good things are always happening for me.

Everything is going my way.

The Universe is surprising me all the time with wonderful, happy things.

Life is fun!

If you don't feel that way, then try on feeling that way!

It won't hurt a thing. In fact, you might find you like it! You might find good things coming your way.

Are you a lucky person?

Someone who believes, "I am lucky" will attract experiences where others will observe and comment, "You are really lucky!"

If you don't believe you are lucky, then realize your point of attraction has matched that belief and feeling.

So start changing that belief today.

Yes, luck is about synchronicity with someone's point of attraction.

But it is also about belief and feeling.

A lucky person experiences greater luck, which reinforces the feeling of being lucky, which expands the point of attraction.

Start today with this simple belief: *I am lucky!*

Then look for evidence.

And watch the fun unfold!

Chapter 14: Releasing Debt

While most of this book is focused on the creation of a prosperity mindset – and vibration – we know that any debt you currently owe can also play a role in how you are allowing yourself to feel. So we would like to briefly address that. If you don't have any debt, then just skip this chapter.

If you are currently in the process of paying off debt, or intend to, then we would like you to consider an intentional shift, from thinking about how much debt you owe to the fact that you are in the process of paying it off (or will be soon).

Energetically, this is a significant shift. You are in the process of paying it off, of relieving yourself of any pressure you associate with debt.

Now, if you feel any of this debt is unfair, that binds you further to the debt. If you resent paying it, it will take you longer to pay it off. So just consider that this is a responsibility that either you assumed or has been assigned to you, but it is yours to pay. And you are in the process of paying it.

Usually, there are minimum or monthly payments to make. Try to make those minimums if you can. If not, then meeting those minimums is on the path to greater prosperity for you.

In the same way that we talk about making money as a game, we want you to lighten up about your bills. And we know that may feel like the impossible if you have debtors regularly contacting you.

Start with an intention to pay. Even if you don't have the ability to pay right now, you can form a solid intention to pay off these bills.

Notice we say "pay off" because it helps if you think that you will eventually not have these debts anymore. Having them is a temporary state.

Try to allow yourself to feel that statement lighten your vibration. Having these debts is *temporary*. You will not always have them. You will eventually pay them all off.

Let yourself breathe.

Debt is a very constricting energy for most people.

So consider that these loans or commitments, through their contrast, have added vastly to the energy of desire which is sitting in your vibrational future. You have created more vibrational wealth in "who you have become" because of your desire to pay these debts off and be relieved of them. They have actually caused strong desire which has added to your vibrational wealth – with which you will eventually come into alignment.

Also, think of these as loans toward your future. You may owe them now, but they are signs first that someone trusted you at some point, which is a good thing. And you are in the process of repaying that trust.

It is important that you feel you take your power back from any debtors, instead of feeling that they have power over you. If you can't make minimum payments yet, be willing to talk to them or write to them to explain your situation and negotiate payments you can actually make.

If they are calling you about payments due or past due, then it is important that those calls or letters or texts don't trigger a fear response in you. You can gradually shift to seeing them as reminders rather than punishments or opportunities to feel berated or unworthy. Work to gradually remove negative emotions from those kinds of contacts. Which means you will likely need to shift how you are thinking about them.

Debt does not mean you are unworthy. Debt usually starts off with thoughts which aren't serving you, which may then become more entrenched patterns of thought and action.

Playing with the idea of credit, originally, likely helped your energy expand, as you allowed the thought of new money and the possibilities of what you could create with it.

Student loans, for instance, are usually taken out with a lot of hope, and the expectation that this is a loan on your future. Loans for education are usually seen more easily as an investment in yourself...until you have to pay them off later.

There is nothing necessarily wrong with loans. They are a cooperative arrangement. They are a relationship. Often there is mutual benefit – the addition of interest, for example, or the feeling from a friend that they are happy to help you.

Later in the book we will talk about thought steps. Work your way up the staircase so you are making peace with your debts, and peace with paying them back.

You can actually learn to feel really glad every time you make a payment.

It will help shift your energy if you see those payments as successes.

If you have ten debts, then try to meet the minimum payments. But pay any extra you can on the smallest debt, to pay it totally off first. Many people will try to pay the bigger debt first, or spread any extra money across all their bills. But it is of more benefit to reduce the total number of debts.

Doesn't it feel easier to think that you have nine instead of ten payments due? That you gradually have six instead of ten? Four instead of ten? Many people ignore the smaller bill because it is less money. Which is precisely why it is the one where you will see progress more quickly.

As you make payments, tell yourself, "I am in the process of paying off these debts. I am reducing the amount I owe every month. I am feeling lighter and lighter energetically. I am allowing myself to come into vibrational balance."

Feel grateful for what you can pay. Put "Love" postage stamps on your bills if you are paying regular mail, and send the payments literally with love. Paying online? Feel love when you click the payment button. Feel glad that you are able to pay the bill. Start to have fun with the paying of bills.

When you have been in a position of not being able to pay, it feels good to be able to pay your bills. It is exciting to watch the amount you owe get less every month. This can be something to celebrate.

Ask for guidance from non-physical about ways to increase your income, so you will have more to pay, more to lighten the total amount owed. You may find that, as you make progress on paying your debts, there is more and more inspiration coming to you about how you can pay them off more quickly.

Energetically, these debts have caused you to ask for tremendous abundance in your life...and perhaps right now you have an abundance of debts. You are going to work on creating an abundance of dollars. You are going to work on allowing prosperity to flow into your life. If you got really practiced at lack of money, you can get really practiced at plenty of money. They are simply different vibrations.

A lot of debt means a lot of energy around debt. So now, you are releasing the debt. You are going to begin instead to focus on the flow of money. And in the same way you created a great flow of debt, you will now create a great flow of money instead.

If words like "debt" or "creditor" evoke fear in you, then play around with these words. Find new words to replace them. Be irreverent. Even dare to be grammatically incorrect! Find other words to use, or ways to lighten these words. Have fun with the language. What other words could you use for "bill" for instance— the "B word" or "William" or the duck? What nouns or adjectives might make you laugh? Don't make it about the drama. Make it light and fun. These topics are just going to be in your life temporarily. Find ways to lighten the mood when they do come up so you can raise the vibration around them.

Life is going to get better for you. Life is getting better for you. Better and better.

You may not have let financial prosperity flow in your life for a long time. As the bills got greater and the pressure of "not enough" grew, so did your attention to it and likely the situation may have gotten worse. You are ready to be relieved of the debt, the pressure, the feeling that there is not enough.

Like trips we talk about taking, this is a journey of releasing debt and allowing greater prosperity. It is a process. But you will find yourself feeling better and better, more and more empowered, along the way, as you allow greater prosperity into your life.

Chapter 15: What is Working

What is working in my life?

Anytime you have a moment where you are feeling less than good, one way to refocus and raise your frequency is to consider: *What **is** working?*

It is easy to pay attention to what isn't working, or isn't working quite the way you would like. So just pause in those moments and ask, *"What is working?"*

What is working with your health? Your home? Relationships?

Your work? Things you do for fun? Your vehicle? The world around you?

From focusing on what is working you can shift and direct your attention higher:

What is working well?

Now, you can step it even higher: *What is working great?* What is fantastic?

If you are having health issues, for instance, it is easy to focus on what is wrong. In fact, that is all the doctors will ask you about. They don't want to hear about what is right – they only want to hear "the bad stuff." But you can focus on what is going right with your body – which is almost everything, if not everything. And it makes whatever isn't working seem more manageable. You begin to see it from a broader view.

If your car needs a repair, of course you will tend to it. But if you recognize that most of your car is still working, then it helps to put the repair into context.

If a relationship in your life isn't where you want it to be, give your attention to any positive aspects in that relationship that are working. If that relationship is in a delicate place for you right now, you may need to leave it out of your field of vision entirely. Don't focus the lens of your mind there. But do find all the other relationships in your life that you enjoy, and think about those – feel those – instead. Find the positive qualities of the people in your life. Focus on the relationships that do feel good.

Maybe you can't pay all your bills this month. But even if you can pay one bill, focus there. Celebrate the bill you can pay. Enjoy how good it feels to be able to pay that bill. If you focus on what you can do – and not on what you can't – then the Universe will help bring you more that you can do.

Usually, when we are not enjoying the abundance we desire, we think that our lives aren't working because we don't have as much money as we would like. If that's the way you're feeling, as you already understand, the law of attraction is going to bring more situations to you that are not working.

Remember that you are like a huge magnet, attracting more to yourself of what you think and feel.

Take out a sheet of paper and start writing down what is working in your life.

If you can find things that are working financially, then note those. Paying even one bill is something to celebrate. Can't pay your credit cards? Shift instead to appreciating that lenders saw you as creditworthy. Have any financial assets? Even one? Celebrate. Note to yourself that there are financial things that are working in your life.

If it feels too triggering to think about money, then leave that off your plate, so to speak. You don't want to activate anything negative or any sense of lack. So focus on what is working, in any and all areas of your life.

Make a list. Bring it out every day. Add to it. Look for what is working in your life.

Every morning, every evening, look at it again. Or make a list all over again!

YOU are a powerful creator!

YOU create more on the frequencies you activate – with what you think about, focus on, and FEEL.

What feels good to you? What is in your life that you like? That you want more of?

WHAT IS WORKING WELL FOR YOU?

No matter what you are living, there is a lot working really well for you.

Find it. Focus on it. Feel it. Enjoy it.

And then watch the Universe begin to deliver to you more like that!

Have fun with all you have created that is working well!

Because the Universe is listening to you all the time. And you have amazing power to create what you want in your life.

Chapter 16: Creating New Momentum

Energy flows.

Energy moves.

It cannot stay still.

Thoughts are energy.

Streams of thoughts are streams of energy.

Thoughts with like frequencies are attracted to each other. That is the law of attraction at work.

Thoughts of abundance cluster together.

Thoughts of lack are attracted to each other.

When you activate a frequency, you will find yourself having other thoughts on that frequency.

Abundant, feel-good thoughts will attract more like themselves.

Lack-based, not-good-feeling thoughts will attract more like themselves.

If you feel bad about something, you will find yourself thinking one negative thought, then another and another, until it seems like you are in a stream of negativity spiraling downward.

But when you think about something that feels really good, it will be easier for you to maintain that positive frequency.

Now, take a moment to consider momentum.

The longer you maintain a frequency, the more – and faster – you will attract like thoughts.

Energy builds as you give a topic more and more attention.

Imagine a mountain.

At the very top of the mountain, there is a spring with beautiful, clear water running.

Naturally, the water is going to follow the path of least resistance, and flow downward, down the mountain.

As the water from this spring flows downward, it is going to merge with water from other springs in the mountain.

Imagine that further down the mountain, the water from these springs have merged into a magnificent, powerful waterfall.

The waterfall is combined springs.

Now imagine each of those springs is a stream of thought – something you have been thinking about for a while.

As the water from these springs flows, so flows the energy of your thoughts. They coalesce, come together, and merge into a great flow of water. And that flow culminates in a waterfall.

Individual springs, like single streams of thought, do have power and value. But as they merge with others like them, they create greater and greater flow. And with the greater flow comes momentum.

The momentum gets stronger with time, with distance.

So goes the momentum of your thoughts.

As you work your way through this book, you will find that you are starting a new spring.

But the patterns of your old thoughts have already created a great deal of momentum.

If you have been feeling lack or shortage or not-enough for a long time, there is considerable momentum that has developed.

So when there is an issue of financial abundance in your life, you must respect that you have developed a great deal of energetic momentum on a particular frequency.

As your frequency about money improves, you will see evidence of it. There may be small signs: finding coins, getting great coupons, receiving a gift or something for free, having a loan repaid to you, winning a prize. This is all evidence you are on the right track.

What happens with many people is that they forget about momentum. You may have years of negative prosperity programming. You likely have some heavy duty momentum going on these issues. You are activating a new spring of thoughts. It will take a while for new momentum to build and catch up to where you want it to be.

Now that you are working on positive energy about financial abundance, you need to recognize it will take a little while to create momentum.

This is part of why it is easier for someone who has lost a fortune to rebuild it quickly. Because they had successful momentum going. They stepped out of that frequency for a while. But they had a lot of momentum going at the frequency of success. So when they are able to find it again, they get back in the energy of that old momentum. It may appear to others that they are starting from scratch again. But they are not. They had strong momentum going, and now they are reaching back into that flow and riding that momentum again.

What often happens when people start doing this work is they see little signs their prosperity is improving. But then some of their old momentum of lack catches up with them, and they feel like they have lost all progress. They get discouraged; they might even feel hopeless.

But all that has happened is that they stepped out of the new momentum they were building into some old momentum that they spent years building...and that no longer represents what they are creating now.

So old momentum is there in your life on these topics.

You don't want to ride it anymore; you want to create new momentum.

The best way to deactivate old momentum is to create new momentum, and stop having thoughts that activate the old stream of energy.

So don't get discouraged when signs of your old momentum show themselves in your life. Just say to yourself, "Oh, that's just old, leftover momentum from how I used to think. I don't think that way anymore. So I am going to let it go, and work instead on my new thoughts and feelings, to build momentum stronger and faster on this new frequency where I want to be living."

Old momentum doesn't define you. But it may catch up with you once in a while, until your new frequency is dominant.

Just realize that it is energy at work. YOUR energy. And you are creating momentum on a new frequency. You spent a long time creating that old waterfall. Now it is time to build a new one.

Be patient with yourself!

Chapter 17: Step by Step

When people think of increasing prosperity in their lives, many people like to envision themselves as very wealthy, even if they are standing in an extreme place of not allowing – a place of real lack. And while there is nothing wrong with doing this, we want you to realize that the path to wealth is a path of many steps.

You have likely been practicing a frequency around money and related subjects for a long time. Because momentum has developed, it would be helpful to recognize that lasting change will require subtle, incremental increases in your vibration.

Think about a situation where someone has a moment of allowing and synchronicity, where they win a significant prize, like the lottery. Now, if this person were offering a vibration only short-term that allowed this money into their lives, they will likely return to their previous vibrational pattern once life settles down. This is why so many lottery winners find themselves returning to difficult financial situations years or even months later. People who have been making vibrational improvement in their momentum and are riding a higher frequency are much more likely to maintain their abundance. But people who have been fearful around issues of money, for example, often find it difficult to release the fear, even when their financial situation improves.

We want to encourage you to think about your situation improving, but to reach for changes that reflect gradual vibrational improvement – real improvement that you can maintain, build on, and where you can continue to move higher as time evolves.

Think about building a skyscraper. A skyscraper needs a firm foundation to support upward growth. The upper floors are not going to be structurally supported if unstable products are used at the building's base.

We want you to consider your thoughts and beliefs about abundance, money, work. We want you to accept that your path to prosperity will get higher and higher, but you are going up one story at a time. Incremental changes may take longer, but they are also more profound and long-lasting.

Moving from a frequency of *lack* to a frequency of *enough* is a fantastic improvement to make. Your quality of life will be enhanced tremendously.

And we know that once you've reached *enough*, you will keep reaching for more. And that's a good thing. Once you have a frequency of enough, it is easier to reach a little higher, then a little higher.

But gradual changes in frequency are more likely to be permanent. So allow yourself to reach higher, achieve more, then reach higher, achieve even more. And so on. Step upward one step at a time.

If a year from now, your current income had doubled, your life would be much better than it is now. You would have more options. You would feel more free, and more secure.

Maybe that feels impossible to you. If it does, then it is too far a reach. Find something more gradual that feels good to you, that feels attainable.

Maybe you don't have any income right now. And even some income would be an improvement.

You need to start where you are; you can't do otherwise.

And then take your thoughts a step higher. And a step higher.

You want to find stability as you improve your vibrational frequency.

Think about a child who is learning to walk. You don't expect a toddler to run a marathon.

At first, a child will stand and practice standing. The child will hold onto something or someone for stability. The child gets used to standing while holding.

Eventually, the child takes a first step. Maybe still holding to someone.

Then the child takes a step alone. And then a second step.

With practice, the child will learn to walk across the room alone without falling.

But this is a gradual process.

Achieving long-lasting financial prosperity is the same way.

Improvements are incremental. And that's a good thing, because long-term improvements in your vibration are more likely to be long-lasting.

Most people find that they clear out old, false beliefs about prosperity later by layer. They get one layer of false beliefs peeled away. It feels great! And they can feel they are at a higher frequency. After practicing that frequency for a while, a new layer of false beliefs appears.

They appear because you have asked: you have asked what is getting in your way.

And the only answer to that ever is: you are.

The life you are living reflects your beliefs, reflects your vibrational offering around money.

It is like going for a college degree. Your first day at your first class, you realize there are many more classes to reach your goal of a degree. But if you are determined to have that degree, then you realize being there that first day means you are on a path to something you really want. It is going to take work; it is going to take time. But you have started a journey toward something that is important to you.

Climbing a staircase means going upward one step at a time.

It is incremental. But each step upward is progress toward where you want to be.

Chapter 18: Thought Steps

Thought steps.

Envision a staircase that leads upward. The upward movement of the staircase reflects the direction you want to move your thoughts and emotions on a particular subject. You want to move the feeling higher, up the emotional scale. You want to move your thoughts on this subject vibrationally higher. You will need a piece of paper to complete this exercise. If the paper has lines, you can let the lines be the steps. Or just draw a staircase on the page.

1) Begin where you are, at the bottom of the staircase. It does not mean you are vibrationally at "the bottom" of anything. You are just starting where you are. Write a statement at the bottom of the page that reflects where you are. Use feeling words.

Examples:

I feel frustrated because I can't get a job I like.

I feel sad because I can't find a relationship partner.

I feel frustrated because I don't have enough money.

Complete this sentence using words that describe how you feel about your present situation:

I feel _____ because/with/by_____

_____.

Place this statement at the bottom of your staircase, at the bottom of your page.

2) Now place a statement at the top of the staircase (page) that reflects how you want to feel and think about the situation. Let go of where you are and think about where you want to be.

How will it feel when you achieve what you are wanting?

If you are having trouble thinking differently, then ask yourself, how does Source — my divine self — feel and think about this situation? You know those thoughts are different than what you are currently thinking because you feel bad about where you are. If you were seeing through the eyes of Source, you would already be feeling better. The negative emotion is an indicator that you are seeing this differently than Source. So...how do you want to think and feel about this topic? Here are a couple of examples.

Example 1: I feel happy because there is an abundance of jobs available to me. I feel empowered knowing I am becoming aligned with the perfect, well-paying job. I feel exhilarated knowing there are lots of jobs out there that are just what I want.

Example 2: I feel excited with the easy flow of money into my life. I am embracing the abundance the Universe is bringing me. The easier I am about it, and the more I trust it is there, the more the Universe brings me. I am full of ideas of how to create more money. The Universe is matching me up with all the resources I need to continue this creation of prosperity for me and my family.

Now complete this sentence using these (or similar) words about how you WANT to feel about your present situation.

I feel _____ because/with/by_____

_____.

Place this statement at the top of your staircase, at the top of your page. This is what you are moving up the staircase toward. This is how you want to feel and think.

3) Now, beginning at the bottom of the stairs, make a statement that feels slightly better than the one at the very bottom. Reach for a thought that feels a little better to you, that brings relief. Write it on the next step higher.

4) Continue to climb up the steps, thought by thought. Write a new, better-feeling thought on each step. If you need to add steps/pages to your staircase, do it! You will know when you have reached the top of the staircase (for today) because you will feel better!

Some key points to remember as you do this:

Write thoughts that feel true to you, that you believe. The stronger the feelings as you write, the more you are shifting the vibration upward.

Put a different thought on each step, then reach a little higher for the next thought step.

You should find yourself feeling better as you move up the staircase.

Here are some sample thought steps on abundance. They begin in different places, but all move to higher frequencies. Some people need more steps than others to think and feel themselves moving higher.

Play around. These are samples. Then write your own, where you can find yourself feeling a little better with each step you take.

These thought steps are written moving from a lower frequency, a lower step, higher up the stairs. If you find one of these samples you can relate to, you will feel better as you read it. If some lines resonate with you, you can use them in your own thought steps.

Sample 1

This is a temporary situation.

I am going to land on my feet financially.

There are lots of opportunities to increase my abundance.

There are many ways money can flow to me.

There are many paths to financial success.

Everything is always working out for me.

Things are getting better and better for me.

The Universe finds many unique ways to increase my financial abundance and well-being.

The Universe is always taking really good care of me.

The opportunities for abundance are unlimited.

My abundance and financial well-being are assured. They are on their way to me and beginning to arrive.

The prosperity of the Universe is abundant, ever-growing, ever-expanding.

I am amassing more and more financial abundance, prosperity and well-being.

I am amazed at the generosity of the Universe and the incredible ease with which money flows to me.

Before I even consciously ask "more please," it has already arrived.

I love knowing the abundance and prosperity of the Universe. I love seeing it in my life. I love experiencing it.

My financial well-being is assured. It is done, and all is well.

Thank you, Universe, for this magnificent abundance!

Sample 2

Financial success is coming ever faster.

My financial condition is improving quickly and easily.

With each passing day, my vibration on this topic improves.

I am happy for others who are financially abundant and successful.

I am making real progress.

It's getting better all the time.

I have an abundance of pleasing things.

I have an abundance of pleasing people in my life.

Financial abundance flows in my personal experience.

The stream of financial abundance flows generously.

I am well along the way.

My increasing abundance is evident.

I am eager and excited as I see my unfolding abundance.

Immediate financial manifestations are occurring.

I am experiencing my natural state of financial ease and well-being.

My success soars.

Sample 3

It's all right.

I can feel that money is coming to me.

I know I am deserving of more.

Now I am figuring out how to let it in.

I deserve to have abundance.

I always have believed I deserved more.

And I have long felt like I had more – just not in the bank yet.

Money is on its way to me.

I'm finding solutions.

There are many solutions coming to me.

There are many opportunities to create abundance.

I haven't missed out. My opportunities are starting to arrive.

Money is flowing to me more and more. My work now is to let it in.

I am letting it unfold naturally.

I can relax into this and figure it out.

I am listening to inspiration and following it.

I am listening to all the guidance coming to me from non-physical – and there's a lot!

And now, I am aligning with it.

Now, I am aligning with who I really am.

I am Source energy, an extension of Divine energy.

I am amazing.

I am loved.

I am worthy.

I am allowing who I really am and what I really want to flow into my life.

And the more I relax and allow and find happiness, the more I can feel that things are getting better and better for me.

More evidence is showing up in my life that I am on the right path.

It was there for me all along, and now, I am aligning with it.

I am letting it in.

I am celebrating who I really am and embracing all the wonderful things about this physical existence.

Life is getting better and better.

I am getting happier and happier.

My work now is to be happy.

My joy now is to figure out how to create more joy, more money, how to allow it in, then follow that passion.

I am feeling happier and happier and I know I am creating new momentum.

Feeling this good about so much in my life means all areas of my life are bringing me reasons to feel good.

All areas of my life are getting better and better.

I love life.

I love being alive.

I love the way the Universe is taking such good care of me.

I love this path I am on, because I can see where I am heading and it is feeling so, so good.

More and more good things are on their way to me, are arriving, and feeling this good is evidence of my new momentum, my happier future, my satisfying present.

All really is well in my world.

Chapter 19: Thought Steps for Business

If you have a business or have/work for a non-profit organization, you will often find that your personal financial situation is reflected in that business or organization, or with your portion of that work. You take your vibration with you wherever you go. Just as your frequency around money is reflected in your personal finances, it also affects your business.

This is one of the reasons we suggest that people do not go into stress-producing debt when they are opening a new business, or extend themselves financially beyond their personal comfort level in investing in their business (or any business venture). If money is tight for you in your personal situation, you want to move up the vibrational scale – improve your frequency – *before* you open a new business, or you will see the same situation eventually reflected in your business as you have been experiencing at home.

The work is vibrational, first.

If you have been struggling financially but then do the vibrational work, you may be inspired to start a new business as you move up the scale. But if your frequency is sufficiently high, then you will also find inspiration for financing the business. Everything will easily fall into place.

If you are not a vibrational match to improvement in a new business, then you will likely find opening it to be a struggle. It might feel like the Universe is conspiring against you, and that everything keeps going wrong. Either you have not done the vibrational work for financial success, or you have not done the work to line up sufficient energy around success for your new business.

Likewise, if you have partners in the business or organization, it is helpful if you are all in a similar frequency of success. The more that the major players in a business or organization are offering a frequency of success, the more everything will come together easily. If you are vibrationally compatible with prosperity, expansion and success will naturally unfold.

If it seems like your business or organization is struggling to be successful, then look first to your own vibration. Work it up the vibrational scale.

If you are offering a strong vibration of success, you will attract people who are a match to that frequency. Don't blame a business partner for not having a high frequency and say that they are the reason your business is not succeeding. Because if your frequency is strong, then either you will attract a partner with a similar vibration, or your current partner – if not a vibrational match to you – will literally vibrate right out of the picture.

Likewise, your personal financial situation may be reflected at work in other ways. If you are a salesperson and work on commission, the higher your personal frequency, the more you will seem to attract customers like magic. You will be offered inspiration from non-physical to improve your sales.

If you are struggling in your personal finances, it may seem like everyone else at work is easily making sales, while you feel invisible to customers. Vibrationally, you are, in effect, invisible to buyers.

If you fundraise for a non-profit organization, you may also see your personal vibration reflected there. The more you are standing on sound financial ground personally, the more you will likely see the organization's development work become successful.

Organizations and businesses don't always understand that if they pay their staff members well so they are experiencing greater ease financially, it will benefit the business as their staff is offering a frequency of success. Add to that the personal energy investment someone makes who actually cares about the organization for which they work. An environment of mutual respect can more than pay for itself with financial rewards in addition to personal ones.

There can be times where someone has conflicting belief systems about home and work. For instance, someone might consider themselves to be a successful fundraiser or money manager, but self-identifies as someone who struggles personally with finances. The outcome will reflect that individual's beliefs.

The tool of thought steps can be used in your thinking for businesses as well as non-profits. We are going to provide a few examples here.

Example for a Non-Profit Organization

The statement at the bottom of the scale, for where one is starting, might be:

I feel anxious because we are financially strapped and money is tight.

For the top of the staircase/page, where you are heading, the aim might be:

I feel joyful because an abundance of money is easily flowing to our organization.

Here are some sample thought steps to move up the staircase.

I believe in this organization. We are doing good things here.

I really appreciate our supporters. We are fortunate to have so many supporters. And we are attracting more all the time.

It's nice that others can see the good work that we are doing.

I am glad to see our membership growing.

More and more people are supporting our organization in many ways, and that feels good.

I know there is enough wealth in this community to financially support this organization.

I know that people can feel good about supporting us, and it is nice that people believe in the work we do.

I know that the more we grow, the more people are discovering the value in us, and want to be partners with us.

It feels good to be associated with such a worthy organization.

I can tell that more and more money is coming to us, more and more members support us, and that we are reaching a place of greater financial ease.

It feels good to see more and more dollars flowing into this organization. And I know that as more dollars flow in, and the more easily they flow, the greater the good we can do in this community.

It feels really nice to see our membership expand, and this organization expand.

I am feeling more and more optimistic about the future of this organization. And I know I am seeing greater physical manifestation of our success.

It's not a dream anymore that we will grow and stand on solid ground. I can really feel that we are more and more stable, more and more expansive. It all feels good and right.

What fun to know that we are growing and expanding, helping more and more, extending our outreach.

I am getting excited about the new possibilities that lie ahead of us, and the evidence I see.

As greater resources flow in, we are flowing out more help and connection. More support in, more support out.

An abundance of money is flowing to our organization, and it is so very, very good!

Example for a Business

For a business which seems to be struggling, the bottom of the scale might be:

I feel discouraged with the financial burden of this business. I am worried that I can't turn it around and make this business a success.

For the top of the staircase, where you are heading, the aim might be:

I feel excited to see this business becoming more and more successful.

Here are some sample thought steps to move up the staircase.

I know that this business can turn around. It's possible. It's even probable. And it's what I am asking for.

I know that when I ask, it's given.

I know that my fears have been standing directly in the way of allowing this business to be successful, and that I am capable of releasing them.

I know that non-physical is tending to the success of this business.

I know that, vibrationally, it is more about allowing success than trying to force it into place.

I know I am in charge of my vibrational offering, and therefore I can change it. I can improve it.

I am a powerful creator.

I like my business. I want to see it grow and expand and flourish.

It's rewarding to see people appreciating what we offer.

It feels good to know others can see the value of my business too.

It's rewarding to see money flowing.

It's fun to come into alignment with the vision I have of this business as a success.

I like being someone who can see the bigger picture.

I like stepping into who I really am and what my business is vibrationally.

I like guiding it into all I know it can be, and vibrationally already is.

I need to get out of the way of my business blooming, and booming. I am here to nurture its growth, not to make it grow.

My business is solid vibrationally, and how exciting it is to watch its success unfolding.

I have always been able to feel this business as successful. It is so wonderful to get out of the way and nurture it to become all it can be.

I am eager to watch my business grow.

I can feel the energy of this business. It is vital and alive and exuberant and thriving.

It feels good to know that all is really well, and that life is getting better and better. This business is getting better and better.

Success is mine. I can feel it. The well-being of this business is assured.

Example for a New Business

When one is starting a new business, it can be easy to lose the momentum of the vision and become ensnarled by details. Here is a sample that might apply to one who is launching a new venture.

The statement at the bottom of the scale, from where one is beginning, might be:

I am worried about starting my new business because there's so much pressure, so much to do, and so many bills.

For the top of the staircase/page, to where you are aiming vibrationally, the statement might be:

I am so happy about all the possibilities my new business brings. I can really feel how wonderful it is.

Here are some sample thought steps to move up the staircase.

I've become so focused on the details that I've lost my vision of what I want this business to become.

I know this anxiety is probably temporary.

I was really excited about this business at the beginning.

I like the idea of being my own boss, and more decisions come with that responsibility.

I like the idea of others partnering with me to make it successful, both staff and clients/customers.

I enjoy telling other people about what I'm doing, seeing them get excited about this business.

It's nice to know others think this is a great idea too.

I think I've just gotten buried in the details, and forgotten about the broader picture of what I am trying to create.

It's not just about having my own business but creating something that benefits others too, and that they can find value in.

It's fun to see my idea become a reality.

My idea was always that this business would be successful.

I think I have been letting my fears run away with me. And I've been listening too much to the cautious advice of others instead of growing my vision.

I think I got caught up in the problems instead of the solutions.

I know everything is always working out for me. I need to tune back into my internal guidance and look for inspiration to follow.

It's nice to know that non-physical sees the bigger picture and can guide me.

I might feel like I am in this alone but I'm not.

It felt really right to start this business. And the way I'm feeling now feels awful, which tells me that Source is seeing this differently.

I am going to get back in touch with how Source is seeing this project.

Source can offer me inspiration and guidance.

I know Source wants me to be successful.

I want to be successful.

I can feel my thinking clearing up, and I'm feeling better and better.

I love being an intentional creator.

It's great to be creating something bigger, something lasting, something that's going to benefit so many.

What I am doing feels so worthwhile.

It's great to see my vision translate into a physical reality.

It's going to be so fun to see this business grow.

I am going to enjoy watching it expand.

I can already feel my pride in it soaring.

I can feel that success is inevitable.

Chapter 20: The Feeling of Abundance

Let's review some of the main points we have discussed so far.

- Focus on what you want, not on what you don't.
- Focus on what you have and like, not on what you feel you lack.
- Financial well-being is yours. Your work is to allow it. And to follow the inspiration which will help guide you to more and more.
- Replace negative thoughts about money with statements of general well-being.
- Affirm the abundance you see in your world and your life. Because abundance is there already.
- Accept and celebrate that the process to more money is easy. It is step after step after step. Divine guidance is with you on the path. Just ask, align, open and allow.
- Your feelings are guidance about whether your thoughts are in alignment with what you want...or not. Find thoughts about money and related topics that feel good to you. Then have a lot of those thoughts! Avoid thoughts about lack, unfairness and other topics that don't feel good. Shift the preponderance of your thoughts to feelings like *enough, plenty, more and more, ease.*

When we use words like abundance or prosperity, many of you resonate that yes, that is what you want. But when we ask you what abundance feels like, you don't have many words for us. When we ask you how you enjoy prosperity, you often tell us what you can't enjoy because you don't have money in the bank yet.

Take a piece of poster board or a very large piece of paper or a bulletin board. Some of you may prefer to do this electronically. But there is something about the physicality of working with the images and seeing them afterward that can help this process.

At the top, write: *I appreciate...*

And then put pictures of things you want in your life. They may be things you have now, or want to add to your life. You are creating your dream life, from your present moment perspective. You can dream as big or as small as you like. A home you love. A vehicle/s. Relationships. Friends. Family. Animals. Travel. Whatever you want.

What things would be in your ideal life?

What places would be in your life?

What people would be in your life?

You may not want to get too specific with people – especially if there aren't physical bodies in these roles yet. Maybe you are single now, but want a loving spouse. Maybe you don't have kids, but want a happy loving family. Maybe you want a dog or cat, but can't have them where you live right now. Don't get too caught up in the specifics. Find images that are symbolic in representing what you want and the feelings you desire.

You want to create a vision of your life, *of what you want*. You also want it to represent not just the things, *but how it feels*.

As you find the feeling of this life you want, write down these feeling words. What does this celebration of abundance feel like to you? How can you elaborate the feelings of this prosperity with words?

Some sample words and phrases might be: *ease, joy, freedom, doing what I love, choices, generosity, living in* (beauty?

simplicity? spaciousness?), *surrounded by* (warmth? family? friends? nature?). You are looking for how this life you want *feels*. Day to day, hour to hour, what are you feeling in this life? (Happiness? Joy? Love? Laughter? Fun? Inspiration? Creativity? Relaxation? Excitement? Satisfaction?)

We can't make this list for you. It is different for everyone. Some people associate abundance with solitude, quiet and peace; others find it amid lots of active humans and animals they love. Some people want exciting, thrilling experiences, where others want calm and relaxation. People want big houses on lots of open land, tiny self-sufficient homes on wheels that can be relocated easily, or small apartments in big cities that are easy to take care of – and everything in-between. Only you know what you want. Only you know how your image of abundance feels.

Some people may have other ways to title their collage. Instead of *I appreciate*, you might prefer writing something like:

- ➢ *I am grateful for...*
- ➢ *And so it is.*
- ➢ *I/we living happily ever after....*

You want to take this life you desire and make it NOW. You want to make it so real you can step into it – that it is no longer your dream, but your vibrational reality.

Chapter 21: An Inspired Rendezvous

An inspired rendezvous is the Universe, through the law of attraction, bringing you together with what you want, or something that indicates you are on the path to what you want. An inspired rendezvous is an indication that you are in alignment – a match to the vibrational frequency of what you desire, of what you find pleasing. An inspired rendezvous is something to celebrate!

An example of an inspired rendezvous is when you are in a parking lot, looking for a place to park your vehicle and you are prompted to pull into one particular space. Then you get out of your vehicle and find money, literally, at your feet.

While shopping in the grocery store, you find the "Fairies of the Universe" have left coupons for you by several items you need to purchase, saving you money.

You have asked the Universe for help in finding a job. You are in line at the cash register at the store and overhear the people in line ahead of you discussing a new position that has just opened up. This job sounds like something you would like, and you are eager to learn more.

You have been working to raise your frequency on abundance and allow more money in your life. Almost everywhere you shop on a particular day, you receive a coupon for a survey to save you a few dollars on your next purchase. Each coupon feels like confirmation you are on the right path.

Having asked the Universe for a piece of furniture that you don't know how you can afford yet, you are prompted to take an unusual route home from work. You drive down a street you normally would not, and pass just what you want sitting out on the curb with a FREE sign on it.

These kinds of situations, which some might call coincidences, are part of how the Universe matches you up with what you desire, when you have achieved the frequency that aligns with what you want. Sometimes they are indicators you are coming closer and closer to the frequency you want – getting within range, so to speak. They are not coincidences. They are synchronicities. It is how the Universe works, bringing like frequencies together.

Happy synchronicities can happen in your life all the time: part of the ease of living in alignment. When you are actively working to raise your frequency on a particular topic, like allowing more money into your life, they can be great confirmation. The work you have been doing, cleaning up your thoughts and feelings about money, is allowing your frequency to rise. They are tangible evidence.

You don't *make* a rendezvous happen. You can't. You attract them into your life easily, because you are a match to what you have asked for. They are evidence of your alignment...and your beliefs.

If you believe you have to work really hard for your money, or that there is a Universal shortage of money, then you are not going to rendezvous with easy money coming into your life.

If you believe that life has to be hard for you, you are not going to rendezvous with a situation that will make your life easier.

If you believe you are unlucky, you are less likely to rendezvous with a win of something enjoyable.

If you believe it is really hard to find a job that pays well, you may not find one easily.

Just as you can rendezvous quickly with things to which you are a vibrational match, you will also prevent yourself from a rendezvous with something you don't believe is going to come easily into your life. Imagine that you have a force field around you, allowing what is a match to your frequency on a particular topic but keeping away what is not a match.

Your beliefs can facilitate ease and allowing, or closing off and difficulty. You can literally prevent, vibrationally, what you want from being able to come to you.

Imagine a benevolent Universe that wants to fill your days with delightful, fun surprises. Each one comes as a kind of confirmation: life is supposed to be good for me, life is supposed to be fun, what I want comes to me easily.

Enjoy the inspired rendezvous, and let them come often. See them as confirmation you are a vibrational match to what you want...you are in range. Have fun with them!

Chapter 22: Activate Happiness

When you give something your attention, you attract more of it into your life...or something on that same frequency. Happy attracts *more* happy. Sad attracts *more* sad. Worry attracts *more* worry.

If you like having an inspired rendezvous, for instance, you could spend time writing down when they happen and how good they feel. As you enjoy and appreciate them, you will find the Universe bringing them to you more and more.

Since being happy will keep you in a high frequency, let's explore some ways you could accentuate the happiness in your life. Being happy will bring you more happiness. And if you aren't having thoughts that will actively keep money away from you, then being happy will facilitate the allowing of more money into your life.

Consider a happiness journal. Find reasons to be happy every day and write them down. Begin your day by writing down what you have to be happy about in your life. You might write down in the morning what you are looking forward to in your day. Before you go to sleep at night, write down some of the highlights of the day that you were happy about, and how you were feeling at the time they happened. As much as you can, record what you were feeling in that present moment.

Make a happy book – a photo book or a scrap book. Put photos and other mementoes in the book of happy moments in your life. Add writing if you like. This is a great project to do with someone you love. It is particularly fun to do with children. You can spend time together adding pages to your happy book as you create wonderful memories in your lives. Or encourage your child to have his or her own happy book. It will help teach the child to look for and celebrate moments of happiness in life...a great habit to develop when young. You can also do this with a mate – record happy moments you are sharing as a couple. You can have a happy book for the relationship if creating it is something you both enjoy, and keep your own individual happy books as well.

Create a happy list. Make a list of 12 or 15 happy memories that always make you feel good. Perhaps it is a list you create in words; maybe it is a digital photo album you keep on your computer, tablet or phone. Put it several places so it is easily accessible to you. When you are having a moment where you are not feeling good, bring out your list. You want to make the list when you are happy, not when you are sad. Even the best memories can be vibrationally elusive when you are feeling unhappy or lonely. Find a time when you are feeling good and make the list. What causes you to smile? What helps you feel good? What makes your heart sing when you remember? Write it down. Make this list physical so it is there when you need it. This happy list will help you feel better when you need it.

My favorite things list. Create a list of your favorite things. They do not need to be things you own now. But the thought of it, the memory of it, makes you feel good. Maybe there is a toy you had as a child, but don't anymore. Thinking about this toy brings you joy. Add it to the list. Maybe it's a rock you found walking someplace meaningful, or when you were with someone special. Things are on this list because the thought of them is valuable to you. The value of the item is irrelevant. Owning it is irrelevant. Whether or not it still exists in a physical way is irrelevant. Thinking about your favorite things makes you feel good. That is what matters. Like children in a thunderstorm recalling things that bring happiness and laughter and chase away fear, remembering your favorite things can be uplifting.

Chapter 23: Happiness First

Finding happiness is not about changing the circumstances of your life so that you then feel good. It is about finding happiness, and then because of your improved frequency, you will find the circumstances of your life improving.

A lot of people say things like, "Well, give me more money and then I will be happy." "Give me a great job, and then I'll be happy."

And we want you to understand, be happy because it feels good. Be happy because it is what you deserve. Be happy because you are worthy of being happy. Because you came to earth in these bodies wanting and expecting you would find happiness. You knew you would create your own happiness.

Once you are happy, you won't worry about money in the same way. You won't be focused on lack or shortage. You can't. They are inconsistent frequencies. You will connect with more options. You will align with solutions. Abundance will come to you more easily.

When writers tell you to do what you love and are passionate about because *then* the money will follow, this is what they are talking about. Many of the wealthiest people on your planet did not set about to make something new because it would bring them wealth. They invented for the fun of it. They explored for the fun of it. They created something new for the fun of it. They worked hard because it didn't feel like hard work. It was their passion. They were doing what felt life-giving to them. They were working hard because that was their happiness, that was their joy.

Are you doing things in your life that bring you joy? Are you spending time with people where you have meaningful conversations? Or the time together feels rewarding? Or you laugh and have fun? Does it feel afterward like time well spent? Do you engage in activities that are fulfilling?

This is not where you go, "I would but..." or "I tried but...."

This is where you figure out how to make it work.

If you aren't having a lot of fun in your life now – whatever that means to you – then start by figuring out one way to add fun. It may be starting an activity, taking a class or workshop, joining a team or league. It may mean carving ten minutes into your day to do what feels good to you. You may have something you have wanted to do or learn for a long time, but you have been putting it off. Don't put it off anymore. Work it into your schedule. If you are lonely, find a way to be with people in a meaningful way. Maybe volunteer your time – perhaps start by helping others who are lonely, giving them some relief, some happiness, through your companionship.

You can receive a lot through giving of yourself to others, if you find that rewarding.

Maybe you feel like you give a lot to others already, and you need some time to focus on what *you* really want – time you can spend on yourself.

Maybe there is something you have always wanted to do professionally, but you don't have the credentials to do it. Perhaps you do have the credentials to do it as a volunteer.

This society, more and more, is removing barriers to people connecting. You can be at home and communicate with people through the internet. You can find videos online to teach you a new skill. If you don't have a computer, you can use one for free at a library or community center. You have access to more information than ever before. You have access to more people than ever before.

It is highly unlikely that someone is going to come, seemingly out of the blue, and hand you something you feel you have been lacking in your life. But it is likely that if you decide to do or be in a new way in your life, in a way that brings you happiness, the Universe will knock itself out supporting you. Your non-physical support team will cheer you on. They will guide you to new opportunities, new ways to make this thing you want successful. But this is your life. You are responsible for your own happiness. You have to make it work.

You need to choose joy.

You need to choose feeling good.

You need to make your happiness a priority.

Children like to make their own fun. That's what play is.

You need to make your own fun.

Don't let it be dependent on anyone else, or on what anyone else thinks.

Don't even tell others about it if you think they won't be supportive. If they won't become your cheerleader on this topic, then there is no reason to share it with them.

Some people who are miserable get upset when they see others around them reaching for happiness. They try to bring those happiness-seekers back down into their own misery. They would rather feel companionship in their misery than see someone – even someone they care about very much – find a joyful life. This is how they cope. But if you choose to stay in misery with them, then you need to assume responsibility for that is a choice you are making.

Choose joy.

Choose happiness.

Find a way to add a little more happiness to your life, then a little more, and a little more.

After a while, you will be less tolerant of negative emotion.

You will be less tolerant of not feeling good – emotionally or physically.

How can you bring more joy into your life?

Figure it out, and start making it happen.

Align with solutions and possibilities.

Allow more and more happiness into your life.

Chapter 24: Activating New Money Memories

There is a story you tell about money in your life: what is it? Has it changed during the course of your lifetime? Is this story serving you?

Many people say the same things about money in their lives year after year. And their situation with money stays the same year after year.

If you want to change your financial situation, you need to change your frequency. Which means moving your beliefs to a higher frequency. Which means moving the story you tell yourself (and others) to a higher frequency too.

The Universe responds to the frequency you offer, not your words. So you need to evolve your story. You need to move your story to a higher frequency. That is why we are saying to move your beliefs to a higher frequency. You need to improve your thoughts about the role of money in your life, about the abundance of it, the availability of it, the flow of it.

Consider the thoughts you repeat to yourself about money every day. One of the ways people often express their beliefs is through the stories they tell themselves, and others, about their present and past prosperity.

Often, people experiencing shortage tell stories of shortage. People experiencing abundance share stories of abundance.

You all have memories in your lives that you associate with abundance – or lack. Repeating stories about shortage perpetuates shortage. It does not matter if they are true. Talking about them again activates that frequency, and perpetuates that same frequency into your future.

What are your key money memories? Do you have memories about money that you replay in your mind, or share with others? Do they create a positive vibration around money? Or do your money memories need to change?

Everyone has positive stories they could tell. But often the stories that seem the most dramatic are about shortage and lack, or winning but then losing. Humans talk more about times they didn't have enough food than times they did have enough; about times they had a shortage of good housing instead of times they had comfortable housing. People are taught to share the dramatic stories – and those usually mean lack, shortage, or loss. People stress the hardship they endured in their stories about overcoming difficulty. If you won something, you may tell the story more about how you lost it. If you had a job most of your life but then were laid off, you may talk about that loss more...especially if you don't have a new job yet. If you lost a home to foreclosure, you may talk more about losing the home than about the good times you had living in it.

Think about the money memories from your childhood. Do you remember finding money? Receiving it as a gift? Or do you remember the times you couldn't afford to buy something you wanted? Or the time you lost something valuable or had it stolen or broken?

The money memories that you think about – that represent the frequencies you are keeping active about money – should be positive. They should create positive feelings within you.

Think about the times in your life that something you wanted came easily to you. You may have to dig into your past a little if you are not used to activating this memory.

Do you remember finding money?

Do you remember someone giving you money?

Do you remember being able to afford buying something you wanted? Or someone giving you something you wanted? Perhaps something your family received that was wanted?

Do you remember getting your first job and being happy about it? Or getting a job that you wanted?

Do you remember someone trusting you? And you feeling that you were worthy of that trust?

Do you remember taking your first trip to somewhere you wanted to go?

If you have a vehicle, do you remember getting your first one? Or one you really wanted?

Do you remember giving someone a gift that was meaningful and pleased them?

Do you remember helping someone out and feeling that your help was really appreciated?

You have all kinds of memories related to abundance, just as you probably have memories of shortage.

Which memories feel better to remember? To talk about? To share?

Society tends to prompt people to recall the worst. But to create the abundance you want in your future, you need to activate the best.

Spend some time actually writing down "My New Money Memories" or "My New Prosperity Memories." Some of the memories may be more about abundance, or helping others, or being helped. They may not be specific to money. But they should all feel good. They should all create a feeling within you of having, of receiving, of giving, of sharing, of earning, of finding, of winning – of abundance being present in your life.

Start re-telling yourself these new memories. Activate them every day. Remember them when you wake up in the morning, when you are stuck in traffic, when you are waiting in line. Recall these good-feeling memories. Let the story of your abundance evolve. Activate new memories that feel good and bring you a feeling of prosperity.

Chapter 25: Choosing Your Perspective

There were many children who grew up during the Depression in the United States in the 1930's who recall that time differently than history books describe it today. Consider this perspective: "I didn't realize how poor we were. We always had enough to eat. We never went to bed hungry. We did a lot of things for fun – they just didn't cost any money. We had lots of freedom and time to spend with friends after school and after we got chores done. I didn't realize until I was older that society considered us poor, because we didn't feel poor. Everyone else we knew was in the same situation. We just thought that was the way life was. And frankly, as a kid, life seemed pretty good."

The person telling this story could choose to focus on how they felt they had enough, how there was an abundance of fun, and how life seemed good.

Or...this person could emphasize growing up during a difficult economic time in the United States, that shortage was common and society viewed them as poor.

The life lived was the same, regardless of the story told. But the perspective taken, the story repeated, and the emotions felt will dramatically influence the frequency this person is offering about his or her childhood. And what is being attracted now.

In any situation, there are multiple perspectives. And the good news is, you get to choose yours!

As you create your new money memories, see if there are stories you have been telling about your past where you can simply choose to change your perspective. Are there any stories about your present where you might choose to shift to a more positive perspective?

Some questions to help you choose a better, higher frequency perspective:

1. Am I sharing my perspective, or the way someone else viewed this situation? I know that other people's opinions used to matter to me a lot – I was a real people pleaser. But what was my own view of this experience?

2. I am trying to figure out how Source saw this situation. If I am not feeling good about it, then I know I am not seeing it through Source's eyes. So how did Source see this? What value did Source find in this experience?

3. I realize now that some of the earlier "lack" I experienced help me to define what was important to me, helped me to focus away from what I didn't want and look instead toward what I wanted. So maybe I need to take the leap and focus now on the benefits that came from that contrast, instead of looking at the contrast that caused it. What did I gain as a result of this experience? Were there benefits to me that have helped me since then?

4. If someone else were telling this story to me, and I was trying to find something positive about it to help uplift them, what would I say?

You can rewrite some past, negative experiences by looking at them from where you are standing NOW. Or by thinking how you would like to view them from the future. For instance, maybe you recently lost a job, but it was a job you hated. So think about the future, when you are standing in a new job that you really like, and how much happier you are there...when you will be saying, "I am so glad to be in my new job. I just love it! And I am so glad I lost that awful old job. It just wasn't a good fit for me anymore."

There are many perspectives to every situation. If you have a story you have been telling, but it doesn't feel good, then either stop telling it or find a new, better-feeling perspective. You get to choose!

Chapter 26: A FUN Process!

When you are in a place of lack as you think about what you want, you are communicating that shortage to the Universe energetically. Remember that your creations are always energetic first. And your emotions signal the distance between your beliefs about what you want and your alignment with achieving it. So if you think about what you want and it feels good, then you are in alignment with manifesting it, and in alignment with how Source is seeing it. If you are not feeling good, then you have thoughts that are out of alignment with Source, and out of alignment with easily manifesting what you want.

If you focus solely on manifesting this thing you want *in the future*, then it will always be in the future. The Universe is reading your energy which says this belongs to your future. As you continue to feel it is coming in the future, the vibrational frequency you are creating perpetuates that it will be in your future, which keeps it from manifesting in your *now*.

You need to realize that you *are in the process* of manifesting what you want. You want to BE this thing NOW. You want to have the feeling of it NOW, as if it already is. You want to enjoy it. You want to have fun with this process of creation.

You want to have fun NOW!

If there is a job you want, we want you to see yourself and feel yourself in it now. How does it feel to be there? How does it feel to wake up and know this is what you will be doing today? Think about your wonderful colleagues. Imagine the great environment in which you are working. Feel the excitement as you are on your way to work. Find the satisfaction you feel on your way home at the end of the day. Imagine what you are telling your friends and family about your fantastic job.

You can do this with whatever you are wanting to manifest. If you want to create your own business, then feel the joy of working in that business. If there is a product you want to manifest, or an artistic creation like a book or piece of art, feel yourself talking happily about it to others after it is done.

If you want to live in a magnificent house, then transport yourself there now, energetically. Feel how great it is. Feel yourself moving around this house and enjoying all its wonderful aspects. See yourself entertaining friends. Think about the fun of decorating, and getting it just right. Or if that aspect is not fun for you, then finding the perfect decorator who seems to read your mind and get everything the way you want it.

Whatever it is that you are wanting, put yourself into the fun of creating it. And experience that fun now. Forget about assigning your project a time when it must be done. Don't look at the fact you don't have it yet. Instead, spend time in your creation, as if it is fully realized. It is already done. Close your eyes and go there in your mind's eye. Feel it. Enjoy it with as many senses as you can.

Feel all the things you love about it. As you find those feelings, think about times you have experienced them in the past. Remember being in other creations – jobs, houses, whatever it is you are wanting – that are like it, that give you the feeling of it. If it is a product or specific thing, then feel that sense of completion, of knowing you made something really fantastic and it feels great.

Make lists of all the marvelous aspects of this creation of yours. So much to love about it. So much to appreciate. Remind yourself of the ease of the process of creating it: once you got into the feeling of it, everything really flowed.

You want to flow energy into the manifestation of what you desire, not into the lack of it.

Every time you realize it isn't there yet, you slow its manifestation. When you activate its absence, you delay it a little more.

We know this sounds contrary to reality. But that is what we are asking you to do. We want you to step out of the physical reality and into your vibrational reality. We want you to focus on flowing energy into your energetic reality, into what you want. And to have fun doing it!

We want you to get so happy and so enjoy the process of creation that you don't realize it hasn't manifested yet.

You want to flow energy into creation of the presence of what you desire, not into creation of lack. You want to focus on the fun of manifesting what you want.

Think about taking a vacation. A vacation can be a lot of fun. But many people enjoy the planning more than the trip. They enjoy looking at all the choices of things to do and how to spend their days. They often make lists that contain many more things than could actually be done during the physical time scheduled. They are excited about it. They look forward to it. They have a strong feeling of expectation. They know this wonderful trip is coming and they are sure of it. They have a lot of fun in the preparation of it, anticipating that the time will come when they will be in the midst of it. They travel in their minds, and find the feeling of this great trip, before they have even packed a suitcase.

That is what we are asking you to do. Find the feeling of this place you want to create before you are there. Enjoy the emotional reality of it before it is manifested.

Some people plan a vacation for months or even years that will only take a weekend or a week in physical reality. But they are there, in their minds and with their emotions, long before the physical reality.

This is the fun "work." This is the fun process.

And remember that the feeling of the process will be manifested with a matching feeling in the physical reality. A good-feeling process can help ensure a good-feeling outcome.

You energetically want to take this vacation before you ever leave home.

Find the feeling of it. Every single day. Get in there and enjoy it. Mentally go to all the places on your list and have fun.

We want you to plan the experience of what you want like you plan a trip. Have fun! Enjoy the process of creation. Live in the feeling of it. Live it <u>now</u>.

Chapter 27: Align with What You Want

Let's imagine there is a far-away destination you have always wanted to visit. Perhaps it is a city or country or famous landmark.

What is your attitude toward getting there?

Many people focus on the reasons they can't get there: I don't have enough money. I don't have the time. I don't have a mate and I don't like to travel alone. I have these health issues. I don't know the language. What if it isn't safe?

But others will align with getting there, align with being at their desired destination. And align with having a wonderful experience. Then they make it happen. They determine that they want to go and they are going. None of the other stuff matters. They will make it work. They are aligned with reaching their destination.

Do you focus on making it work, or on what might get in the way?

Do you find reasons that you may fail before you have even started your journey, or do you focus on a successful outcome?

Are you aligned with what you want? Or are you focused on resistant thoughts that create obstacles in your path?

Consider how it will feel to reach your destination. What are the feelings you would equate with success?

Then consider the feelings of resistance. In the example mentioned above, dominant feelings include fear, lack, shortage.

The Universe is responding to the thoughts and feelings you have about reaching your destination.

Is your energy aligned, or is it wavering?

If you were to set off to the grocery store today, you would expect that destination to be reachable because it seems realistic to you. You know it is achievable.

Do you consider the other things you want achievable?

If you determine, for example, the far-away destination to be the trip of a lifetime, that adds a lot of pressure to it. That adds resistance.

But if you decide this is where I am going, it brings relief.

A lot of people end this physical experience without reaching the travel destinations they want to visit. And that's okay, because they visit once they reach non-physical.

If your destination seems really far away, it may mean it is far away from where you are standing right now vibrationally. Or else you would be planning that trip – or would be there already.

There is nothing wrong with having a big destination. But allow yourself time to get there. And we don't mean just in the physical miles, but in the vibrational miles. If where you want to go seems far away, then there are likely many vibrational steps to getting there. Which is fine.

But remember to look at where you want to go. Not on how many steps or miles are between you and your destination. Not on where you are standing now. Each step you take can bring you closer to what you want.

Another question to ask yourself is: am I clear about what I want? Or am I confusing my destination with the journey there?

Here is what we mean. Some people who want to be wealthy – yet aren't standing there in this moment – decide they want to win the lottery. And we say, do you want to win the lottery or do you want to be wealthy, and that is the only path you see there? Is winning the lottery the destination, or just one possible path to your destination of wealth?

If the destination is wealth, there are many paths there.

If you decide to allow greater abundance to flow to you, the Universe will help you get there as you allow it.

But if you decide there is only one path there, you are closing off many doors that might help you reach your destination sooner.

So be clear about your destination.

Then think how you will feel in reaching your destination.

Sometimes, people will decide to reach a destination, but not think about how they want to feel when they reach it.

For instance, maybe it is only important to you that you reach it. You don't think about how you want the journey there also to be a marvelous experience. How great it is going to feel when you have arrived. How you are going to embrace every moment with gusto.

Do you just want to get there, or do you want getting there to be fantastic?

What is the experience going to be like once you are there?

Pick the dominant emotions you want on your trip, and you want once you arrive.

Be clear. Label them.

Then start asking yourself: how can I bring those emotions more into my everyday life? How can I experience them more now, without waiting?

There is a huge emotional component to reaching your destination.

If reaching the destination feels achievable, then you have already started to get there.

What other emotions will be part of this wonderful journey? What will it feel like when you have arrived where you want to go?

Then start bringing emotional aspects of your destination into your life now.

Everyone's destination may be different. But we know that for most of you, it will feel great. You will relish reaching a place you have wanted to be. You will feel vital and alive. You will feel successful. You will be exuberant. You will be having fun. You will feel you are thriving. You will be joyful.

Make the feelings of your destination real.

Pause for a moment in your reading, and make a list of how it will feel.

Make the list in the present tense, as if you are there now.

But more importantly, <u>feel</u> the list in the present, as if you are experiencing it now.

Then start looking for, and creating, opportunities to bring those feelings home, into your life, now. Every day.

The more you feel them now, the more you become a match to your destination.

Start simply.

Take the one or two feelings on your list that you think you can find more in your life every day.

Start there.

Figure out how these can be themes for you.

For instance, let's say you pick the feeling of success.

Every time you complete a task in your life that you want or need to do, even something as basic as laundry, acknowledge to yourself: *I got it done. I was successful in doing what I wanted to accomplish. I am a success. I am a successful person.*

Start looking for opportunities to congratulate yourself.

I went to the grocery store and found almost everything on my list. It was a very successful trip.

Find ways to enjoy a feeling of success throughout your day.

Look at the past, at times you were successful. Because there were many times you accomplished something you set about doing.

Start a list. *My past successes...*

End each day as you go to bed thinking about the successes of your day.

Let success become a theme in your life.

Let it become a dominant theme.

Maybe you go, "Well, I can do the laundry but I can't pay the bills...."

Can you see how that last thought impedes the progress of success?

If you feel successful in other areas of your life, then eventually that frequency, that vibration, will start to flow over into all areas of your life.

Maybe you can't pay the bills today. But if you start recognizing that you are successful in other areas of your life, then is there really any reason you can't be successful financially too?

Perhaps you can start to soften that, and think, *I am successful in many areas of my life, and I am starting to be successful financially too. I can feel success coming there. I know that being a successful person is who I really am, and that success is flowing into all areas of my life.*

Doesn't success feel good? Doesn't it feel empowering? Doesn't it feel freeing? Don't you feel capable? Don't you like the way you feel when you think of yourself as successful?

Whatever feeling you choose as your theme, embrace it. Practice it.

You need to be intentional about it, especially at first. You need to practice it on purpose.

But once you get some momentum going, you will find evidence easier to come by. The law of attraction will start working with you to bring you more evidence of your success, more feelings of success, more thoughts of success.

Soon, you will find people telling you how successful you are, how great you are at accomplishing something. Yes, this is a person who determines to do something and gets it done. Yes, this is a successful person.

Chapter 28: Am I Asking the Right Question?

Often, people ask questions like, how can I create greater abundance in my life? How can I attract more money? But often, the real questions that lead to the creation of more abundance are the questions preceding those. What questions will lead you to the right answer, to the layer of frequency that is where your real *change work* needs to occur?

For instance, trying to create more abundance in your life if you still have core beliefs that resist money will yield you lots of frustrated effort.

Why do I not have more money in my life now?

What beliefs do I have, if any, that have kept me from attracting what I want?

Sometimes, the answers to these questions are very simple.

Perhaps you think you must be worthy to have money, and you do not feel worthy.

Perhaps you resent rich people (which means you don't want to become one). Or you believe it is harder for people who are rich to get into heaven.

Perhaps you were taught to equate money with evil…and you still have remnants of that belief.

Perhaps you think you can't become abundant without an educational degree or particular certificate or license.

Perhaps you have a hard time imagining yourself as successful.

Perhaps you see yourself as someone who has messed up too many times.

Perhaps you don't think of yourself as deserving.

Maybe you think money is hard to get, or to get legally, or other people have money but not you.

Maybe you think you have to work really hard for decades to earn sufficient money.

Maybe you think you have no one to inherit money from, and that's the only easy path.

Maybe you resent paying taxes, and are glad you're not in a higher income bracket where you would likely pay more.

Maybe you feel guilty if you have money but those around you do not.

Maybe you were told earlier in your life that you would never be rich and you better get used to it, or that having enough money is a lifelong struggle.

Maybe you believe that if you come into money, having it will be temporary and unsustainable.

Maybe you believe life isn't fair.

If you have been wanting to be more abundant for a long time, there may be some questions you need to ask yourself and resolve before you ask how to attract more money.

When were the first times you experienced "not enough" and did you interpret them to mean something about you or your life? Did you internalize that feeling and think it meant something about you? Did you accept that money was always going to be a struggle, or grow used to the feeling of *not enough*?

Did you accept the beliefs of adults or others around you? A parent? A teacher? A boss?

Did you somehow come to believe you were not worthy, or were only worthy of struggle and hardship?

Spending a lot of time on these questions may not be helpful. If the process is going to bring you down vibrationally, to a lower frequency, then it is not beneficial. But if you look at it more as solving a mystery, then finding the right question can help lead you to the right answer.

Not having abundance may be the manifestation produced by other beliefs you hold about money, yourself or your life.

So ask *why* a few times. See what comes up for you.

If it feels deeper or more complicated energetically, then you might want to take out a sheet of paper and brainstorm some of your own beliefs about money. Then about you having money.

If you envision yourself financially successful, how does it feel? Does it feel great, and is the vision really clear? Or does it feel muddy, like something else (in your belief system) is messing up with a brilliant picture of a successful you?

Find the right question.

Any belief you unearth can be transformed so that it doesn't continue to hold you back – if you are willing to do the work. That's the great news. You don't have to worry about what you find, because you can change it. You can make it better. You can move yourself to a higher frequency on that topic. And maybe this chapter doesn't apply to you at all, and you can simply move to the next chapter.

Don't be afraid to look deeper, to find the right questions. Don't struggle there – don't look too long. Let your emotions guide you. But if you were to act as sleuth for a while, within your own belief system, are there other questions to ask? Are there new answers to find?

Remember:

You are not broken. There is nothing wrong with you. There is nothing unworthy about you.

But maybe, just maybe, some of the beliefs you have held about yourself are broken.

Maybe some of the beliefs about what you are capable of are broken.

Maybe some of the beliefs you have about your own success and wealth potential are broken.

Those are what needs fixing.

Not you.

Because there is nothing wrong with you.

You are worthy of success.

You are worthy of prosperity.

You are worthy of joyful living

and a joyful life.

You are worthy of love.

You can fix broken beliefs, beliefs that are false to their core.

Hollow cores are easily broken
and then repaired,
made stronger
so they stand up right,

so they stand up on their own.

You can't build a strong building
on a faulty foundation.

So if there are false beliefs, broken beliefs,
in the foundation of what you believe,

then you need to find them
and fix them.

Fix them by finding the truth about you
as Source knows it to be.

Fix them by seeing the worthiness in you

and how tremendously much
you are capable of accomplishing in your life.

Fix them by finding alignment with who you really are,
instead of repeating false beliefs to yourself
that never had any truth to them.

You need to create new thoughts
that embrace the incredible value you have
and celebrate it.

You need a mindset that reflects
who you REALLY are
and what your potential truly is.

You need beliefs that accurately reflect
your value, your worthiness,
your powerfully-flowing stream of prosperity.

Happy you. Fulfilled you. Joyful you. Worthy you. Loved you.

Living an abundant life

as big as you can dream.

You were never broken. There was never anything wrong with
you.

Embrace your worth,
your true worthiness,
and find the stream of your real value,
the real flow of your prosperity.

False beliefs can keep you in a false stream.

But the real you,
the "you" that you recognize in your heart
as who you truly are:

don't keep that person in the shadows anymore.

Bring the real you
out of the darkness
and into the light

so your true brilliance

can shine.

Chapter 29: Changing Topic-Specific Patterns

Let's look at long-standing frequencies: patterns of thought about particular subjects. Imagine there is an amazing trip that you have always wanted to take. The opportunity to take this trip comes up every year. Perhaps the trip is offered by a group. Or you have an annual vacation and think every year about this place where you would really like to go.

Every time you think about this trip, you plan to take it the following year. You start off with the intent. But then something goes wrong. You never seem to save enough money. Or you save the money and then a major expense arises that requires your vacation funds. So you postpone taking this wonderful trip year after year. You continue to want it. And you continue to regret that you have not figured out how to take it.

Now, the trip used here is just an example of a topic about which you may have developed a long-standing pattern of feeling and thought. "I want it, but I can't have it." "It's too expensive for me." "Something always seems more important to spend the money or time on." These are just a few examples. "I want a new car, but I can't afford one." "I want to buy a house, but I can't save the down payment." "I want a new job, but I am too young/old, or too experienced/inexperienced, or don't have the right credentials." "I want to start a business but I don't have the initial capital." What is the story you have been telling in your life about something you have been wanting for a while? (And have not been manifesting....)

First, it is important to identify the topic where you have this pattern. It may not take you long to identify one or more of them. You will find repetition: you want it, don't have it, want it, don't have it. This pattern has been occurring for an extended period of time.

That repetition means you have a long-developed frequency on this topic. A frequency of wanting it and not getting it. You might be feeling frustration around this topic, or disappointment, or maybe something stronger, like resentment or anger.

A long-standing pattern also means energetic momentum. When you have thoughts about this topic, you activate the energetic "baggage" that comes with it. You think about this topic and do not feel good. You no longer feel excitement or eagerness. Instead, the feeling that dominates is negative emotion. You have a stream of energy flowing on this topic, but the momentum of the stream does not serve you.

Since you created this stream, however, you can also change its frequency, its direction.

First, you identify the topic.

Then, you identify the pattern.

Third, you identify the emotions that the topic now evokes in you.

Let's go back to the example of the trip.

The topic is the trip you have been wanting to take.

The pattern is that you set an intent to make it work every year, but then something gets in the way.

The main emotions are frustration and disappointment. And increasingly, a feeling you may never get to take the trip.

So let's work on changing the pattern.

Think back to the emotions originally associated with this topic when it was first desired.

The trip would be fun. It would be exciting to see new places and meet new people. The trip would be relaxing and energizing at the same time.

Now, name the emotions first felt. In this case, it might be excitement. Eagerness. Fun. Happiness.

Are these emotions you have in your life now, to any extent?

If they are, that's great. You want to spend more time in those emotions.

If those emotions feel far away, then start thinking about how you can create them in your life, even to a small extent. These are emotions you want to grow. You want to start experiencing positive feelings about this trip each day in your life.

Create a new intention to start activating those emotions in your life every single day.

With time, the positive emotions will grow stronger. The momentum of those feelings will increase.

But to start, think about how you can bring those emotions into your life, even if just for a few minutes every day.

Maybe you start by identifying something in your life you can feel eager about every day. Some people love their jobs and are eager to go to work. Others are eager to come home, to see their children or partner or animals. What can you add to your life to allow you to feel eagerness and joyful excitement? Or where do you have that feeling already, and you can identify it and make it stronger?

Where is there fun in your life? How can you build fun into your life every day? If it is not there already, then start a list of fun things. Start working them into your life.

Whatever the feelings are that you associate with having what you want, try to identify them and give them a role – or a bigger role – in your life.

When you have the feeling in your life every day that matches what you want, then you start offering a frequency that matches you *having* this subject, instead of lacking it.

Don't make the feeling of having what you want unreachable. Saying you want your "dream home" or calling a job you want "the achievement of a lifetime" adds a lot of extra baggage and weight…and actually adds resistance to the flow of energy.

You want to make this topic real: within your grasp. You want it to seem achievable, allowable. Don't make it too big.

"Thought step" your way there. Take this trip, and think yourself up a step at a time until it feels real.

For instance:

I know this trip seems really big to me.

But I know that it isn't a big deal to other people. So maybe it doesn't need to seem so big to me.

People take trips all the time. They can figure out how to afford them.

If they can do it, I can too.

I can save a little every week.

I can take on extra work to save for this trip.

I can figure out how to add a little extra income to my life.

The extra work doesn't have to be hard or take a lot of time.

I know I can be good about saving money.

It will be fun to watch the money grow.

It will be fun to see the trip getting more and more real as I save.

I know I can ask the Universe for help. I can ask my non-physical support team to offer me inspiration about how to earn extra money. And maybe I can find other ways to allow extra money to flow.

It's going to be fun to know I am on the path to actually manifesting this trip.

It's going to be fun to think about it and plan it.

Even now, I am starting to get excited.

This trip is starting to feel real for the first time.

I can feel it start moving into my reality.

I am starting a notebook today with how much I am saving.

I think I am going to open a new bank account just to put my trip money in.

I am starting to get ideas about what I can do to bring in a little more money.

I am going to start following-up on those ideas right now.

I bet I can have my first money in that account within two weeks.

And won't that be fun?!

It's not just about taking the trip anymore. It's about building the account to take the trip.

Every bit of money I earn and deposit I am going to feel so good about.

They are all steps on the journey to what I want.

And the journey there is going to be fun and exciting, too.

I am starting to feel really eager about making that first deposit.

Oh, this is going to be fun. The journey to my trip is now something I am getting excited about.

The vibration about the trip has now changed to eagerness, fun, excitement.

It is no longer just about the trip as a destination, but the journey to the trip will be enjoyable too.

Feel how the frequency has changed with these simple thought steps.

The thought journey can lead to improved feelings which will uplift the frequency.

Then, action begins.

In this case, the individual is opening to inspiration for new ideas to create money for the trip.

Action is important.

With inspired ideas, it feels good to follow through – to create, in this case, more opportunities for income to add to the trip fund.

You may have heard the phrase that hope is not a plan.

You can hope something will work out – hope is good!

But then you need to follow up on the feeling of hope with inspired action.

Remember that the Universe has unlimited resources to support you, to help you get where you want to go.

And you have access to infinite intelligence.

So when you know what you want, find a way to feel that it is possible...probable...even likely.

Or that it is a *YES!* And that *no* is not an option.

Ask for inspiration. Get into a good-feeling place where you can allow yourself to receive it.

When you find inspiration that feels right, follow it. Take action.

And remember: the journey to something that feels good should feel good, too.

Chapter 30: I Did It! Celebrate Victories

As you climb your way up the financial scale into greater abundance, it is important to acknowledge your progress and celebrate victories.

Just as you climb a staircase step by step, you will begin to achieve one victory after another. They may seem small at first. But acknowledging your progress and growing abundance will help to attract more prosperity into your life. Because now you are affirming your growing financial success.

No one leaps from shortage to prosperity in one swift movement. People who win the lottery the first time must improve their vibrational frequency or they will return to where they were financially before the win. Even then, the win can remain an advantage if they choose to focus on the fact that they manifested the money once, therefore they should be able to do it again. Because it is easier to do something a second time than a first – and easier to believe in your ability to do it.

A child in school who routinely gets As on a report card doesn't have trouble believing he or she can earn an A in a new course. But a child who usually gets Cs can find it much more daunting to think about getting that first A on the next report card.

Climbing your way up the financial scale can sound like a lot of work. But it is more about allowing your natural well-being to flow to you. Then affirm that greater flow as it enters your life. The effort is, at first, to improve the way you think and feel about abundance in your life, to gradually allow your frequency to rise.

Consider the athlete who decides to run a marathon. The athlete doesn't set out to run 26.2 miles the first day – and won't make it if attempted. The body and mind must train.

Marathon runners routinely say that the greatest challenge in completing a marathon is first mental, then physical. They see completing a marathon as evidence of mental discipline as much as physical condition.

You are training your mind. You are learning to think a new way, a better way. But you must focus. You must discipline yourself not to have "old" thoughts or get back into ruts created by previous patterns of thinking.

That is why celebrating victories is so important.

Imagine driving down a muddy dirt road in the country. The first vehicle driving that road after heavy rain storms will help forge a path, driving around big puddles and any other obstacles. The second vehicle will see that first vehicle had success from the tracks in the road, and usually stick to the path already created. The third vehicle will ride those same tracks and deepen the impressions.

Vibrational patterning is like that. Creating something new takes time, effort, more focus, greater awareness. The second time is a little easier, because there is already a path. Subsequent trips down that road will get easier each time, as the impressions are already created. New paths are emerging, becoming stronger and clearer.

Early victories may not seem significant financially, but they are indicators you are creating a new path. Acknowledging them is affirmation. You are affirming your new path, and deepening the new tracks.

Sometimes you hear entrepreneurs talk about how the first sale meant so much more to them than the thousandth. The first sale was affirmation they had a worthwhile product that someone wanted to buy. The thousandth sale was continued affirmation of that path. But the first sale felt much more meaningful. They remember it.

It is the reason shop owners used to frame the first dollar bill they received in their store and would hang it on the wall: that first sale meant a great deal.

Early victories are important.

Affirming the first sale can help lead to the thousandth.

Celebrate "I did it!" moments. Affirm your wins.

Even small victories are important, because they help create the patterning that will allow greater ones.

Your winning steps leading up a stairway to greater prosperity.

Congratulate yourself, and enjoy the feeling. Expand the feeling by celebrating. After all: you did it!

It is important to celebrate your victories. Even small early wins.

AND...

1. Celebrate them for yourself. And only with others if they will see them as meaningful as you do.

2. Do not practice the school of thought that goes: something good happened, so now something bad must happen. Like the saying that you are now "waiting for the other shoe to drop," meaning that if something good happened, something not-good must happen next. And something not-good must happen before something else good can happen again. If you continue to celebrate your wins, then with law of attraction, you will attract even greater victories.

3. Don't spend a lot of money celebrating early wins. It is not about the size of the celebration: it is about the size of the

feeling of success. You want to expand the feeling of success and accomplishment. Some people will spend more money congratulating themselves than they received through their victory, and feel like they ended up digging themselves deeper in the hole financially. It is the size of the *feeling* that matters – your celebration should be an affirmation that expands your feeling of accomplishment.

Have you ever shared news of a win with someone, only to have been told that it was a fluke, or you just got lucky, or the person offered you lots of admonitions about lurking failures? It's like going to the doctor and being told a condition is cured. And you share the good news with your friends and instead get stories about someone they once knew (or distantly heard of) who was cured of a condition and then it came back...or they got something worse.

These are the kinds of friends you may not want to spend a lot of time around as you move your frequency higher. Because they are not supporting you in your ascent. They may be well-intentioned. But they are not compounding your frequency as it climbs higher – they are not affirming it, or you.

Some friends and family may grow resentful as you become more prosperous. Sometimes, they worry you will change. Others worry you will grow away from them. Some people like company in their misery. If you are not miserable any more, maybe you won't want to spend time with them. Or maybe you will think you are better than they are. Maybe they will think you are better and feel inferior. Maybe they will resent that you are practicing self-discipline and improving yourself. Maybe they would rather you were just all suffering together and staying on a frequency familiar to them.

This is not true love. It may be what some people call love. But it is not unconditional love and support.

When you really love someone, you want them to be happy. You want them to be successful as that individual defines it. You want your loved one to find alignment with who they really are.

But some people can't offer that from where they are currently standing in their lives. Usually because they haven't felt it themselves for a long time. So don't blame them for not offering it to you. Just move gently, and lovingly, away, continuing to hold the best vision of them that you can.

It is better for you to know of your victories and celebrate them alone, than to share the news with someone who will not support your high frequency. If you are not feeling better after sharing the news, then this was not the right person to share the news with, at least not at this time.

You will develop an intuition around this, if you have not already. Who will lovingly support you, and be genuinely happy for you? If you don't have enough (or any) of those people in your life right now, that may be something you want to change.

Likewise, you can consider how you feel when people share news of successes with you.

Are you truly, unconditionally, happy for them?

Or do you feel something else? Are you a little resentful? Do you have misgivings?

Time for you to clean that frequency up.

When someone is successful, it is evidence that people can do it: people achieve success all the time.

The more you see people achieving success, the more it can affirm for you: "People *are* achieving success. There is an abundance of success in this world, and people are allowing it.

And this news also affirms I am on a frequency to attract news of success. Which is also a really good indicator.

I attracted a great story of success.

I attracted more evidence that success is abundant.

I attracted someone who was able to achieve it.

And this is all supporting the belief that I can do it too.

I AM doing it too!"

Chapter 31: Their Opinions Don't Matter

Many people who have been struggling financially have come to let the opinions that others have of them matter. Too much.

Maybe you feel you are not as successful or formally educated as other people in your life. You have let yourself feel inferior.

Maybe you feel they look down on you – or you look down on yourself.

Maybe you feel like you have screwed up too many times.

Maybe you feel you have let friends and family down.

There can be many ways in which you have come to let the opinions of others influence your opinion of you.

And that can be a problem.

Because it may feel like the world is watching as you try to rise.

And that the people closest to you are judging you.

Maybe you worry about how they will judge you.

Maybe you are already judging yourself harshly.

Or maybe you worry about how others will see you if you do succeed. What if you make more money than your friends and family? How will that affect your relationships and your life?

If you are used to spending time with people who make fun of those wealthier than they are, do you really want to become one of the others? Would greater abundance cause you to feel like an outsider?

Have you come to let the opinions of others have much influence on you?

As you climb up the steps to greater abundance in your life, it is important that you let all of this go. Release it. Because if you are carrying their opinions with you, then it is like climbing stairs while you are carrying them on your back. All that extra weight will either slow you down, or keep you from being successful at what you want to achieve.

You need to get into alignment with you: with the fullness of who you really are. With what you want in your life.

And you need to leave all the others out of it.

Perhaps you have wonderfully supportive people in your life, and this chapter feels irrelevant to you. If so, that's great.

Maybe you have people in your life who say all the right things to you. But it feels a little off somehow. Like they aren't saying to you exactly what they believe.

This journey you are on is a journey between where you are now, and reaching the fullness of who you really are. Reaching the potential you can feel inside you.

Because even if you have moments of doubt, you can feel that things are supposed to be better for you. Life is supposed to be easier. Money is intended to flow freely.

You know that. You can feel that.

Source knows that. Source wants that for you. Source believes in your ability to get there.

In fact, Source is calling you there. Source is calling you to the next step, and the next step, and the next.

So, are you going to listen to Infinite Intelligence? Or to the people who have been down there in the muck with you, having practiced their own resistant thinking for years?

Who do you think really knows who you are? Who knows that essence of success inside you?

Who are you going to listen to?

You might love these people a lot. But leave them out of it. Release their opinions and expectations. Let them all go.

This is your journey, not theirs. They can climb higher, too. They can choose to begin a new journey. In fact, your success might be inspirational.

Chapter 32: As You Rise, You Inspire

If you know that "a rising tide lifts all boats," then you know that as you rise, you are also bringing up others.

You are setting a model for others to follow. You are showing them it can be done.

You are going to provide hope to people you care about, people who love you.

Because as you rise, you inspire them.

If you can do it, they can too.

And if they don't want to, or choose not to, or if they have already risen – it doesn't matter. Because this journey is yours.

You're not doing it for them. You are doing it because it is who you are. You can't stop yourself from doing it. Because rising is what you do. Thriving is what you do. Becoming more and more of who you really are: that's what you do.

But as you rise, you lift others with you.

Don't take that as responsibility you must bear. Because it isn't yours to carry.

It is your joy to see others rising. And to know you have helped to contribute to it through your own success.

Follow your path as your heart calls you to it. As you know it to be.

Because by allowing yourself to fulfill more and more of that potential you know is inside you, you are also going to model for others how they can align with their potential.

Think about someone who has been struggling with money for a while. They rise, and no longer struggle. That is great inspiration to someone else who is currently standing in a place they used to be.

If you had a mountain to climb, wouldn't you rather hear from someone who has already climbed it? Who once stood where you are, at the bottom of that mountain, then successfully climbed all the way to the top?

Or would you rather hear from someone with no experience climbing mountains?

Part of the challenge in the climb is believing you can do it. Then knowing that you can do it, that you will do it, that you are doing it.

Many people stand at the bottom of the mountain and want to climb it, but then talk themselves out of it.

Not only can you get there. But when you do, it will inspire others that they can too.

A rising tide lifts all boats.

As you rise, you inspire.

Chapter 33: Master Your Internal Dialogue

You understand by this point that the only person who can keep you from being the amazing, successful person you really are is you. You are the only one who can prevent you from reaching the success you intend. That's the good news. You have the power. No one else does.

There are a few basic tools to apply to this process. They sound simple. But like many things that sound simple, they can be challenging to master and to implement consistently.

It's good that you're up for it!

1) Focus. You must become disciplined in focusing on what you want, and stop paying a lot of attention to what is – especially if you don't like what is. Of course you need to pay some attention to what you have currently manifested in your life. But if it is not reflective of where you want to go, then make sure it doesn't dominate your thinking. The Universe will bring you more of what is a vibrational match to you. If you are focusing on shortage or lack, you will attract more of those. So just realize that what you focus on is being broadcast on the big screen – and the entire Universe is responding.

2) Internal dialogue. You are talking to yourself all the time. You feed yourself thoughts about what you want, and whether or not you believe you are capable of manifesting it. Even if you are kind to other people in your life, you may be unkind to yourself. You have to become your own best friend. You have to support yourself unconditionally. Become your own censor. Censor thoughts that are unkind to you. Push the pause button and find thoughts that are better, that are supportive. Don't take criticism from yourself, about yourself. Clean up your internal dialogue. Be loving toward yourself. Support your

worthiness. Choose positive thoughts. Choose thoughts that align with the real you and what you want. Be your own cheerleader.

3) Become the master storyteller of your life. Learn to tell the best stories about yourself – not the worst. Look for stories that affirm what you want to manifest more of in your life. Then share those stories. Stop talking about anything that doesn't align with what you want for yourself. Find the positive aspects of your present. And your future. Share those.

You can talk about what you want as if you have already manifested it. Manifest the FEELING of it. Your feelings come in response to your thoughts. So if you are feeling great, it means your thoughts are in alignment with who you really are.

4) Get happy now. This is the piece of advice that no one wants to hear. You need to get happy. Now. Because, no matter what you are living, being happy now ensures a happy future. This is not "pretend" happy. This is *real* happy. The Universe knows the difference. Vibrationally, there is a huge difference.

If you have not been happy for a while, then before you experience happiness, you may simply find relief. If you are used to being in a lot of pain, for instance, less pain brings relief. It indicates you are on the right track. So a move from *hurting a lot* to *hurting less* to *almost not hurting* to *not hurting at all*: that's real progress!

Only you know what your path is like.

Be careful not to equate relief with joy. Feeling relief is not the same thing as feeling great. Reach for feeling better from wherever you are. There is tremendous improvement in that. Then keep reaching to feel better. And better. Until you get to happy. Then reach for more happy. And more. And more.

Because your happiness does matter.

Don't settle for less.

5) Follow inspiration. Because as you become a better cheerleader for yourself, and spend more time focusing on what you want, you will find inspiration coming to you. Listen to it. Follow it. True inspiration will feel good to you. It may be a whisper, or it may be shouting at you. But it will feel good. It won't tell you anything bad to do, or something that is harmful to someone. It will feel inspiring and uplifting. It will bring ideas that evoke excitement. You won't be asking, "Should I do it?" You'll be saying, "It was impossible not to do it."

Inspiration from Source never hurts anyone else. It uplifts. It encourages and supports.

You will have ideas that feel so good to you, you get excited just thinking about them.

6) Take action from alignment.

Align with what you want. Align with Source. Then take action.

Pushing yourself into something means there is a lack of alignment. When you are aligned with doing something, it will feel right. You have probably heard the saying, "Feel the fear and do it anyway." It is much better to get in alignment first so there is no fear. Maybe there is emotion because you are taking steps in a new direction; you are creating a new energetic path. But the path should feel right...even if you don't understand why it feels right.

You are the creator of your life experience. Allow yourself to be the master creator you naturally are.

Chapter 34: Be Happy Now

Money doesn't bring happiness. *Oh, you say, let me try finding that out for myself: maybe it does!*

Money doesn't bring fulfillment. It doesn't bring love. It doesn't give meaning to your life.

A lot of people are waiting until they have more abundance in their lives to be happy. Because they equate greater wealth with happiness. They want more money because they think it will make them happy – or happier.

There is nothing wrong with wanting more money. But it is not the solution to greater joy and meaning in your life.

Yes, you can certainly have fun creating greater abundance in your life.

Creating greater abundance can be a fun journey.

But don't expect abundance to be the answer to any emptiness you feel in your life.

Don't expect that your life will all of a sudden be much better just because you have greater prosperity.

There are lots of miserable rich people.

Yes, it's wonderful to be able to pay your bills.

Yes, it's great to feel there are more choices in your life that money can allow.

It's a good feeling to help others financially because you easily can.

But what is more important is to figure out

how to be happy now.

Because your life, your daily experience of living, *is now*.

Your power, your joy, is in the choices you make today. Now.

What most people find is that if they are happy now, and then create greater abundance,

they are happy <u>and</u> have greater abundance.

But if they are miserable, and have greater abundance,

they are still miserable.

That's why you want to stop waiting for money to be happy...if you have been waiting.

You want to stop waiting for money in order to feel fulfilled... because they are not the same thing.

On your path to greater prosperity, you need to figure out

how to be happy now.

What can you do to bring greater joy into your life, every single day?

What gives you pleasure now?

Most of the meaningful joy that people experience in life has nothing to do with money.

For many people, relationships bring meaning and joy – relationships with people, with animals, with nature, with Source.

For many, the creative process is fulfilling – whatever it is that you like to create, whether it is home, family, work, music, sports, the arts, vehicles, gardens/yard, cooking, writing, building, hobbies – whatever you love to create or make, or through which you express yourself.

Whatever brings joy and fulfillment into your life, try to spend more time doing those things.

When you are happier, and your frequency is higher, then you will more easily attract abundance into your life.

When you feel an abundance of love, meaning, happiness – then an abundance of dollars can flow to you more easily, too.

Don't wait for money to get happy.

Get happy, and the money will more easily flow.

Chapter 35: Feeling Successful

Success means different things to different people. Only you can define what it means to you.

Some people like to think back to the kind of life they envisioned for themselves when they were children. Many people, when they were young, envisioned the life they wanted as adults. That usually included an assortment of things like a spouse, children, animals, a career, a home, a vehicle.

Others knew they wanted something different. They had other dreams for themselves.

As children, most people have a sense of at least part of what they want when they grow up.

Do you have any of the things you wanted as a child for your adult self? Even if you don't have it in this moment, have you been able to experience any of the things you envisioned? Consider it successful if you have, even if you don't have it now. Consider it successful if you consciously made other choices. Or if you have managed to find happiness in whatever your life experience has been.

There are many kinds of successes. But that feeling of success is important for everyone to claim and know.

Make a list of some of your successes. Take time to reflect on your accomplishments. Everyone has them. Sometimes, they are measured through relationships with people. Sometimes, it's as simple as practicing kindness. They may be things you did, but they may also be qualities you are.

Think of yourself as a successful person – regardless of where you are financially in your life. Then look for evidence to support that understanding.

Consider starting a journal or notebook to document your successes – past and present. If success is not a feeling that comes easily to you, then you might want to take a few moments to write down each night what successes you experienced that day. They do not need to be big accomplishments – whatever feels meaningful to you in your life. Getting the kids to bed on time or with all homework done, having clean laundry and dishes – those kinds of stepping stones are part of the pathway to feeling successful in your daily life.

You want to feel that things are always working out well for you. And if that feeling is not yet coming naturally for you, then it helps to find support each day for that belief. The more you truly believe – and feel – it, the more it will become true for you in all areas of your life.

Chapter 36: Partners in Success

If you are not yet used to thinking of yourself as successful, then it can be helpful to find partners with whom you can practice successful thinking. Success is a mind-set. It is important to develop a consciousness of success in how you think about yourself, your life, your present and your future.

You might find a friend you can sit and share success stories with once a week. Or start a Support Success group where you gather with other like-minded people periodically. You don't have to meet in person – so many options are available now to to meet online or talk on the phone. But in-person is great, too!

The purpose of these meetings is to share stories of success. This is different than bragging. Often in our lives, we are taught to be humble and not talk about our successes. It is okay for others to share good news about us, but we are often discouraged from telling others when we have accomplished something.

If you recognize that EVERYONE has successes in their lives, then it starts to become more acceptable to share your good news. We all have good news. Our society, and often our families, are focused on sharing what went wrong. With your partners in success, create opportunities to share what is going right.

Sometimes, it takes practice to start looking for what is going right in our lives. We are so used to talking about what went wrong at work or school, we don't talk about all the things that went right. We talk about our troubled relationships with family members or friends, but not about the great times we had with them, or the relationships that are easy and going well.

The format for these Support Success gatherings is easy.

First, you must *all* be committed to staying focused on success. It can be easy to stray off-topic, and you need to help bring each other back to success when someone starts wandering. You may not be used to talking about success and it can be challenging to stay at that frequency until it becomes well-practiced.

It helps to clarify a few ground rules up front. If you have a group that meets regularly, you may want to remind everyone at the beginning of the meeting, and/or have a list posted in the room that everyone can see.

1) Only positive talk allowed.

2) No judgments. Do not judge yourself or others.

3) Don't discredit what someone else considers a success; success is personal.

4) Don't talk over each other, or talk at the same time. Allow the speaker to finish.

5) Each participant should spend about the same amount of time talking.

6) If you are going to say anything about what someone else has shared, it should be brief and uplifting. But the group may also decide that group members will only listen when it is not their turn to speak.

7) No advice is to be given unless someone specifically asks for a piece of information. And advice should be shared at the end of the meeting – not in the middle – as it can shift the frequency and tone of the encounter.

If you have a large group, you might want to begin with a timer. For instance, everyone talks for five minutes. At first, some people will have trouble finding topics for five minutes. But develop this as a group responsibility. Each person SHOULD talk for five minutes before the group ends. This will encourage each person to look for successes before the next meeting to fill his or her time.

It is okay to bring a list. If you have been keeping a success journal, it would be easy to bring and share from there. Or you might take a moment before the group starts to allow people to write down their successes for that week, and think what they want to talk about during their five minutes.

If some people talk significantly longer than others, having a timer or timekeeper is very beneficial. The role of timekeeper could rotate around the group. If Person One is the speaker, then perhaps Person Four is the timekeeper. Then the roles pass clockwise with each person taking a turn.

Another technique which can be helpful is to have a neutral item in the center of the table, or that all group members have in front of them. If someone starts speaking negatively or becomes problem-oriented, you simply take that object and lay it down in front of him/her. The object might be something as simple as paperclips or candies – or consider what the group might find fun, like bubbles or balls. You can also do this if someone begins to offer unsolicited advice or a negative judgment of another person's success or situation.

This is not meant to place blame in any way. It is easy to become distracted and fall into old patterns. This is a gentle way of reminding the person to become intentional about what is being said. Sometimes people speak faster than they mindfully think.

As you try out the five-minute time period, or whatever group members agree on, you may find you need to begin with an even shorter time period – maybe three minutes. You may start off with shorter meetings until members become more practiced at talking about their successes.

If you are meeting a friend for coffee, you might begin with one or two successes each, and just take turns. One person shares a success, then the other, and you just keep alternating.

Sometimes, when one person shares, it will remind you of something else you can talk about when it is your turn again.

Remember that this is not about competing or comparing your successes with anyone else's. This is about getting in the habit of recognizing your successes and talking about them. It is creating a safe and supportive environment to practice a success consciousness. Everyone is at a different place in their journeys. You don't want to compare your successes to anyone else's, or use the group as a chance to "beat yourself up" because you feel others are having more success than you. The measure of success in this group is not the content shared, but the time you spend practicing as you talk and think about success. You are growing your frequency of success, and learning to look at the world to find the successes you and others experience.

If you have a group meeting, one option for closing the meeting is to ask if people have intentions they hope to realize before your next meeting. Be aware that some people may have intentions that are very personal, and they may not feel comfortable sharing with the entire group. Likewise, you may ask group members to keep these intentions confidential. Sharing intentions for success is a nice way to close, and to get people to practice intentionally thinking about creating success. Let members know, however, this sharing of intentions is to think about turning desires into firmer intentions. There should be no sense of shame if the intentions have not been realized at the next meeting. And some intentions may clearly be more long-term.

Another option for closing the meeting is for people to genuinely congratulate each other on the successes shared. Appreciate each other and what has been brought to the group.

Chapter 37: The Path of Least Resistance

As you practice success consciousnes and get more momentum going on this higher frequency, you will begin to notice changes in your life. At first, some of them will be quite subtle. Things will seem to be going the way you want them to more often. People will sometimes treat you a little differently – a little better. You may find greater ease in your life, or what you ask for coming to you more easily. You may find yourself busier as you begin attracting more and more of what you want. These changes may appear quietly, gently at first. But as you start to take notice – and your momentum builds – they will become stronger and clearer.

There may be activities you enjoyed, or at least participated in, in the past that are no longer as appealing. Some of the people in your life may change, as your frequencies no longer resonate in the same way. You may find new activities and interests calling you.

These changes may be different for everyone. But it helps to be mindful of them.

These changes are feedback, in response to your improving vibrational frequency. They may not always feel good. Some of them may bring confusion. But much of the time, they will feel great! As what you attract to you is shifting higher, the Universe is affirming for you that your active frequency is rising.

As you gain confidence that you are offering a frequency attracting – and allowing – greater success to come your way, it helps to consider the path of least resistance.

Sometimes, you might determine you want to take a specific course of action. But it seems like the whole Universe is lining up to prevent you from taking that course of action.

Instead, another door opens. A new opportunity presents itself.

You might be so determined to stick with your original course of action that you miss the Universe arranging an even better option for you.

It's okay to change. It's okay to be flexible. If one door is stubbornly refusing to open for you, it may be that it's the wrong door.

If another door appears and opens easily, it is worth asking yourself if that is a better match.

The door that opens easily – that has less resistance – may be the one leading you to what you really want.

Imagine the inventor who is in search of a very specific invention – and comes up with an even better one instead!

Or the business idea that doesn't work...but leads to one that *is* highly lucrative.

There are always alternatives. The Universe lines up one opportunity after another for you when you offer a frequency of success.

There is no such thing as your *one*, your *only* chance.

If you do "miss" one, the Universe will bring you another. And another.

If, however, you believe you somehow missed the one opportunity that would forever improve your life...then that belief can deter you from aligning with other opportunities.

Unresolved issues around money can affect the unfolding of your success. Which is even stronger reason to deal with those issues and improve your thoughts and feelings on topics like finance and prosperity.

If you believe life has to be difficult and a struggle, it will be.

It you believe you have to work really hard to be even a little successful, then that's what you will live.

If you believe you aren't worthy of wealth, then financial success will continue to elude you.

If you believe you have repeatedly been treated unfairly, then that's how you will continue to be treated.

Your life mirrors your frequency...and your beliefs.

Align your beliefs about yourself and your life with achieving what you really want.

Once you begin to feel that alignment, enjoy the Universe affirming your higher frequency.

Allow the Universe to offer you friendly detours that may get you where you want to go even sooner.

Don't turn away from the path of least resistance because it seems like the easier path – because it seems like it happened too easily or too quickly. Or because you are so focused on the destination that you won't allow a newer, better pathway there.

There are lots of paths there.

Look for paths that feel inspired, that feel like they are calling you.

Open yourself to pathways that evoke passion from you. That feel really, *really* good to think about.

Just remember there will always be more paths, more doors.

Opportunities for you are limitless and unending.

Part of a consciousness of success is determining that you are successful, and you will be successful. It is who you are. No one can keep it from you.

If the first door doesn't open, then that's not your door. Just start looking for the next one, because there is always a next one...if you allow yourself to see it.

Life is going to continue getting better and better for you.

Now isn't that wonderful?!

Chapter 38: Desire

The stream of prosperity is abundant and unlimited.

The stream of prosperity flowing to you from Source is boundless. There is not a finite, limited supply of resources. It is constantly expanding. What is available to you is constantly expanding.

You may have been taught growing up that there are limits, that there is only so much prosperity to go around. But that's not accurate. Just consider how the stock market continues to grow and grow. It has expanded already more than many people thought possible – bigger than many could even dream it to become.

Because you have something does not mean that others cannot have it too. Because others have it already does not mean that you cannot.

The resources of the Universe are infinite and continually expanding. What is available to you is also constantly expanding.

Doesn't it feel great to know that?

When you were a child, you may have been taught to share a toy. Not because it was the kind thing to do. Or the fun thing to do. Not because it would have been fun to play with someone else, co-create with someone else. But because there was only one of this particular toy to play with.

And in that moment, you birthed a desire: you wanted your own toy to play with.

What we want you to understand is that it would have been okay for you to have the toy and for your playmate to have the toy. It was okay, in that moment, to want two of the same toy. That was not a "bad" desire.

Since you probably only wanted that same toy for a few minutes, it may not have been logical to have more than one. But it was fine to want what you wanted.

You are constantly birthing desires. And that is a good thing.

Your desires are thoughts, are new creations of energy. They contribute to the overall expansion of the Universe.

You are hard-wired to have desires.

If you never desired food or water, you wouldn't be here as a physical being right now. Your body needs food and water to survive.

You need sleep – opportunities to tune to Source, refresh and release resistance.

It is impossible for you not to want things. Wanting is good. It is essential to your survival.

As basic needs are met, you start to want more things, greater things.

Instead of just wanting food to not feel hungry, you want food that helps you feel good, that tastes good.

Many people find great satisfaction in the creating and eating of foods that taste ever-better, that help you feel ever-better.

Of course, eating food from a state of alignment is the greatest food pleasure. And allows your body to access easily the best of it.

Chefs may say that creating delicious food from a state of alignment is their greatest food pleasure.

You cannot stop desiring. You cannot stop wanting.

You may have learned to curb your desires if you believe you can't get what you want. But even then, you are desiring to desire less, because you believe the unfulfillment of your desires doesn't feel good – so it makes sense to not want what you believe you can't have.

You will always have desires. And that is a good thing. The expansion of the Universe depends on it.

Chapter 39: A Consciousness of Abundance

Consider what you may be feeling a shortage of in your life.

Money?

How about time? Space? Health? Happiness? Privacy? Love? Meaningful relationships? Children? Animals?

If you affirm for yourself regularly that you are lacking one thing in your life, that affects your point of attraction.

A focus on one point of shortage will bring you more points of shortage.

If you feel like you have too much stuff and not enough space, you are feeling shortage of space. Which means you are emanating a feeling of shortage. Of restriction. Of resistance.

Maybe you feel like you don't have time to do everything you want to. And you feel this much of your day.

Perhaps you feel a lack of freedom. Abundance is a feeling of freedom and ease. So feeling restricted throughout your day can affect your point of attraction.

Is there something you are feeling a shortage of, a lack of?

We don't mean financial prosperity.

A consciousness of abundance means you find abundant time, space, relationships, vitality to do what matters to you. There is enough for you to fully enjoy your life. And then from *enough*, to *more than enough*.

If you are feeling a heaviness in your life – a heaviness of stuff, body weight, people you care for, jobs you go to and don't like, things to do, things you must do – then you are not feeling ease and freedom.

And that can affect your point of attraction on topics like money too.

You can't feel heaviness and freedom at the same time.

Now, you can take almost any subject and find a way to think differently about it, better about it.

You can thought-step your way to a better feeling place.

Even if you are incarcerated, you can find ways to feel free within the space that you have. You can use your imagination to think *free*, to feel *free*. Your mind can soar to great heights as a bird while you sit on the cot in your cell. You can experience many wonderful adventures without ever physically moving.

If you are a parent chauffeuring kids around hours each day and that is stressful for you, then you can find ways to make it fun, to make it meaningful to spend time with these children who mean so much to you. To be outdoors where there is so much to appreciate. To have the freedom and comfort your vehicle provides.

If you feel burdened by all the stuff in your house, and that it takes a lot of time to maintain, you can consider how many people would find joy in those very same things – and give them to people who would appreciate them. You can trust that if you need something in the future, the Universe will make it available to you. You don't need to hold onto it all now, in the present, because of a possible *future* need. Trust your ability to create what you will need in your future. Place more emphasis on having things in your present that enhance your life.

If you feel shortage of things where you are living, then, instead of shortage – consider this as room for expansion. This is room to invite and evoke life-enhancing, joy-producing items in your future – and what fun that will be.

Almost any situation that produces a heaviness or feeling of lack in someone can yield a feeling of lightness and "having" in someone else. It is all about perspective.

You control the perspective you bring to yourself and your life. How you look at others. How you see the world.

What areas In your life, that you experience or think about daily, bring feelings of restriction, heaviness, shortage or lack?

See if you can begin to find ways to bring feelings of lightness, abundance, freedom, and ease into how you are thinking. Realize your own power to choose. Begin to feel better. And better. Move into a greater consciousness of abundance.

Chapter 40: Happiness

We invite you to embark on a three-day *Mission Possible*, when you focus on one positive emotion related to abundance each day.

If we were to tell you that everyone in the world could be happy, you would find that possible, because you know there is not a finite supply of happiness. Happiness *is* available to everyone.

If we were to tell you that everyone in the world could be laughing at the same time, you would not disagree and say that only a certain amount of people can be laughing at any one time.

You know that the emotion of happiness is abundant and easily available.

You likely have many more thoughts of resistance about abundance than you do about happiness and laughter. Oh, you may have a few on those subjects. But if we were to weigh resistant thoughts, we think the scale would be heavier with your stack of limiting thoughts about prosperity.

So think instead about happiness.

And if you are not happy in this moment, think about the simple path to getting there: feeling better.

You know you can feel a little better. And then a little *more* "better."

You have had moments of happiness in your life. You can recall them, and think about some of those same moments every day to feel better.

One of the ways people find themselves laughing the most is when they are surprised. They are surprised by something someone says or does. It is the unexpected delight.

Leave the topic of money aside for a while.

Focus instead on happiness.

The same universal principles and laws apply to the creation and attraction of happiness as they do to prosperity.

But you may believe that it is easier for you to create some joy in your life today.

You may think about talking with someone who makes you laugh. Or watching a funny video, television program or movie.

You may think about a dog or cat or baby who is so adorable that they just invite you to be happy as you watch them.

You know happiness is abundant. And if you become determined to find happiness in the world, you can do it.

If you decide to attract greater happiness into your world today, you can do it.

This is your *Mission Possible* today. Go into the world and find happiness. Find laughter. Find people who are enjoying a moment in time.

We assure you that it is possible. And that if you decide to focus on happiness today, you will feel better. You will get out of your own way, so to speak.

Notice we are not saying "look for happiness." We are saying "*find* happiness." *Find* has a definitive quality of success to it. It means you *are* connecting with happiness today.

Maybe you become the impetus for someone else to find happiness today. Maybe you instigate laughter by telling a joke, or being silly, or doing something unexpected. Maybe you share a funny video with a friend or colleague. Because as you find happiness yourself, it becomes easy for you to share it. And the sharing prolongs and expands your own joy.

Chapter 41: Freedom

Just as we want you to spend a day finding happiness, we want you to spend a second day finding freedom.

Pick a day – today or tomorrow works well – and dedicate the day to finding freedom. Look for people and animals who are feeling free – who experience moments of freedom throughout their day.

They might be dogs running in the park. Children playing at a playground.

It might be you playing on your phone at your job, when your boss thinks you are working.

Look for the birds flying. They feel free. They feel so free that sometimes they like to fly just for the fun of it – not because they have a place to go.

Think about any transportation available to you, and where that could take you.

Think about moving through dance or yoga or sports – stretching your body in gentle ways, fun ways, strong ways, healthy ways.

Think about taking a moment from your desk at work, or your chair at home, to close your eyes and envision the most beautiful place in the world.

Think about kittens and puppies who scamper around because they feel free and are so happy enjoying the vitality of their bodies.

These are just some thoughts to inspire your own imagination.

You are free to make choices each day. Hundreds of times throughout each day, you choose.

You are born free. Your minds are born free.

No matter what you are living physically, you are free to use your own imagination, to think what you want to think.

Sometimes, people who don't have great freedom of body find – create – much greater freedom of mind.

You are all free. You are as free as you will allow yourself to be.

Today, find freedom.

Chapter 42: Ease

On the third day of your *Mission Possible*, we want you to find ease.

Throughout your day, look for moments when things happen easily. They don't take a lot of effort. Maybe they don't take any. Maybe you have a thought and, a little later, what you wanted appears without any effort whatsoever. It simply came to you because energetically you asked for it.

Look for things to fall easily in place today. Look for answers to come to questions quickly – maybe even before the question has fully formed in your mind.

Expect to have moments of inspiration, where you are one with the guidance of the Universe easily directing you to something to make you smile.

Expect ease. Find it. Feel it.

Your life is supposed to be easy. It is supposed to be a whole lot easier than you allow it to be. So today, you are finding ease. And allowing more of it into your life.

Ease is allowing.

It is developing an expectation that what you want comes easily, without a lot of effort.

Look for stories of ease – of people telling you how something seemed to unfold magically.

Or how they thought something would be difficult and it wasn't at all.

They thought they would be late, but the event hadn't started yet. Or their boss didn't notice when they arrived at work.

They thought a destination would be hard to find, but it was like the place was lighted up, calling to them.

They got a parking spot right away.

They got an unexpected discount on a meal.

They went to the store, and a coupon for the exact product they wanted was next to it, on the store's shelf.

The mechanic knew right away how to fix their car. And gave them a good price.

Ease.

It comes in many forms.

It just takes being aware – noticing it is there.

With time, you come to expect ease in your life.

It is not just that everything is always working out well for you. Everything is also unfolding easily for you. Life unfolds easily for you.

You don't "make" ease happen. You can't. Then it's not ease!

You allow ease. You create ease through clarity of focus.

Imagine a big glass jar with hundreds of brightly-colored jelly beans in it – jelly beans of many beautiful colors. We say, "Find the red jelly beans." And you gently direct your attention to the red ones. It's not work. You are simply tuning to the frequency of red jelly beans. And finding them easily.

Find ease in your world today.

Today, celebrate ease.

Here are some caveats to your *Mission Possible*, and your three topics.

Focus on one topic each day, not on three topics in one day.

Begin with the one that feels easiest to you. Or find *happiness* on day one, *freedom* on day two, *ease* on day three.

You want to fully activate, and find, the positive feelings and thoughts of your topic of the day.

You might find some carryover. For instance, you might see even more happiness on your day of freedom. Enjoy that. That is evidence of you working with the law of attraction. You activated happiness on day one, so it is logical there would be some energetic momentum carrying into day two.

If you attract some negativity on these topics, just release it and redirect your attention to the subject positively. The law of attraction might be responding to another frequency you are offering – even on another topic. For instance, there are people who say freedom comes with a price. Or life is supposed to be hard, not easy. If you attract energy contrary to what you want, just release it. Don't beat yourself up about attracting those thoughts. Just gently redirect your focus to what you do want to be thinking about. It's not a big deal if you encounter a little negativity along the way. You are an intentional focuser – you know you get to choose where you direct your attention. Be an unconditionally positive focuser: persist on finding thoughts that feel good. You don't need to convince anyone else – that's not your work.

Find happiness,

Freedom,

Ease.

In your life, all around you.

Let those be your red jelly beans.

Chapter 43: You Are the Sun

You are the center of your universe.

You may have been told as a child that was not true.

But of course it is true.

How could it be any other way?

You generate a field of energy that affects the world around you.

You are the sun.

You are what everything else in your world is revolving around.

You determine all of it.

Never underestimate how powerful you are,

or how much of your world you are creating.

You are creating everything that is in your life.

That is the great news. And the challenging news.

Because we can hear some of you going, "I would never have created *that* thing in my universe."

And we gently, lovingly, say: Yes, of course you did. Or it wouldn't be there.

But we also say, there may be carryovers from when you were not *intentionally* thinking, and not *intentionally* creating.

There may be – even a lot – of carryovers from when you were responding to the world,

instead of initiating,

when you were living in response to what others were creating.

There may be topics at the fringe of your experience that are the result of mass consciousness, not your individual consciousness. But you don't need to give them much attention.

So take yourself off the hook for what is there that isn't wanted.

Contrast serves you tremendously well.

When you go into an ice cream shop with many flavors of ice cream, you know from your accumulated experience what you like and what you don't. You know if there are new flavors in this store that you haven't tried yet. And depending on the names of major ingredients, you also draw from your experience. Maybe you really like chocolate, for instance, or vanilla. Maybe you don't.

There is no right or wrong. Because you are the center of your universe. You get to decide what works for you.

Everyone gets to decide what works for them.

Everyone is the center of their own personal universe, the creator of their own life experience, their own reality.

It's just that most people don't know they are.

And you do.

Chapter 44: Priorities

As the sun in your own life, you choose what matters to you. And then, hopefully, you direct your focus there – you shine your light on what matters most.

If you have not intentionally been directing your focus toward your priorities, you may want to spend more energy deliberately focusing.

There are many ways to attract abundance into your life.

Two of the most common are: 1) doing what you love and are passionate about, so that you feel good most of the time; 2) accumulating money is a priority in your life; money matters to you.

Many people want enough money – or more than enough – but they don't spend a lot of energy actually making the accumulation of money a priority.

Your bills might be a priority. But many people approach bills from a place of lack, not from appreciation that they have money to pay them.

Many people choose a career or job without considering what they will earn to be a priority. For instance, people might choose a career because it seems like it will be fulfilling to them, or allow them to travel, or allow them flexibility to make their family a priority. The majority of students in college are not making a career choice simply because of how much that profession pays.

Likewise, you might spend more time thinking about spending money than accumulating it. You might like to think about shopping more than saving or earning.

There is no right or wrong here. But your life tends to reflect your priorities, meaning where you have directed a lot of your attention.

If you are finding an imbalance – more money going out than coming in, for instance – it may be a reflection of where you have been directing your attention. As you come into vibrational balance, financial balance will follow.

Many people with lots of money are very frugal – at least about some things – because they like to save money. Maybe they don't see many reasons to spend money. Or they feel like their basic needs and desires are met.

Others may have a strong flow of money coming in and going out.

Most millionaires do not look like the stereotype of someone with wealth. They may not have lots of new clothes or cars or big houses. Because they don't see the need for it. What they have is comfortable and has served them well. They would rather save the money, donate it, or spend it on something more meaningful to them.

In the eastern United States, there used to be a differentiation between "old" money and "new" money – meaning those whose families had been wealthy for a long time, and those who had newly acquired wealth. The people who were "flashy" with their wealth were often those with "new" money. They were not used to having money, and had not reached a consistent frequency of comfort with it. They showed it off, instead of just "living" with it.

One of the advantages of stepping up, financially, over time, is that your frequency adjusts as your wealth grows. You are more able to maintain a steady increase. You can handle the flow.

Consider children in elementary school being introduced to the principles of mathematics. You aren't going to take children from a basic arithmetic class and move them to trigonometry the next year. Their comfort with math, understanding it and knowing what to do with it, will increase gradually as they study and get a better grasp of the knowledge.

Likewise, when people win the lottery, many seek financial and legal advisors. They know they are stepping into new territory – into an unfamiliar vibration – and they want to draw advice from people with more experience at that frequency.

You don't have to be focused on the accumulation of money in order to attract a lot of it into your life. Many people who are wealthy did not set out with that intent. But if you are feeling a shortage of money, you might ask yourself if accumulating money is important to you. Is it a priority? How much of a priority? Is spending more of a priority than accumulating? Saving? Giving?

Money is a vibrational currency – it is energy that flows. If you allow it – and don't resist the flow – then it can flow easily into your life.

You might also consider: how much of a priority is the accumulation of wealth? Do you seek an easy flow in, an easy flow out? Do you want more so you can save it? Give it away? Spend it? What would represent balance for you in your life? Consider what balance would *feel* like. Security? Freedom? Ease? Flow? Generosity?

Many people find great joy in accumulating and saving money. Many find great joy in growing what they have so they can give it away, so they can share with others and support causes and organizations that are meaningful to them. Many want to grow the money in their lives so their children can have more than they did.

You may say to us, "But I work many hours each week at a job to earn money." There are not many careers where your attention at that job is the creation, the accumulation of money. You may be busy working at the tasks of your job. Those tasks are your main focus. You likely are not focused on accumulating more personal wealth – even if you are aware of how much you are making per hour or day. Careers such as finance tend to focus more on money. But even then, many workers are focused on making money for others, rather than accumulating personal wealth for themselves. And as they handle money for others, they may be the first to find fear if the stock market loses points or something else happens that feels out of their control – something that can affect the earnings of their clients.

Consider what your financial priorities are. Allow a balance. A balance will occur naturally, with internal guidance, if you allow it. When you come into vibrational balance, you will find financial balance.

Envision how water naturally flows and finds its balance. Too much water – too much flow of one energy – creates a flood. A great lack of water – too little flow – creates a drought. Eventually, nature balances it.

While water may flow in and out, also ponder the concept of a reservoir – a place to hold water. Many people are not just concerned with the intake and outflow of money, but also with the holding of money. Holding might mean savings or investments, for instance – a place for money to grow. Expand your thinking, if you have not already, beyond the accumulation and spending of money – the stream coming in and flowing out – to also consider the reservoir.

Your non-physical support team knows what resources you have coming in, and what money will be going out. They see the flow of energy prior to the physical manifestation. Listen to them. Listen to your internal guidance. Ask them your questions. They can help guide you to a state of balance.

Chapter 45: Generosity

When we bring up the subject of generosity, some people flinch. If you are already feeling a shortage of money, you might worry that we are going to tell you to give what little you have away.

Don't worry – we are not.

We would never tell you do to something with money with which you cannot align yourself.

We would never tell you to do something with money that would increase your feeling of shortage.

However...

generosity is one of those subjects which can sneak up on you and increase the flow of the energy in your life, without you being aware of it.

Consider the topics that spring to mind when most people feel a shortage. Money, yes. But also time. Space. Relationships. Fulfillment. Shortage can seep into many areas of your life if you allow it.

When you feel you have enough of something, or more than enough of something, it is easy for you to share it – to give it away.

When you share something – when you give it to someone else – it creates a stronger flow of energy moving through you.

So when you give *time* in your life to someone else, or to an organization that can benefit from it: 1) you are feeling a sense of enoughness, or more-than-enoughness, and 2) you are creating an opening in your life and energy field, as you allow the sharing, and offer the gift, of the time you have.

Generosity is powerful. It is a powerful way to move energy. It is a powerful invitation to the Universe to bring you more.

You are also, energetically, telling the Universe that you are willing to help be the conduit to others of what they are asking for, but are not yet in a position to personally allow into their lives.

For instance, someone may feel such a shortage of money that he cannot earn enough to buy food. Yet he can create an opportunity to eat at a shelter or soup kitchen that will give him the food he desires and needs. His feeling of shortage around money keeps money at a distance. But volunteers who donate their time to help create meals for people in need become a path of least resistance. This man is powerfully asking for help. Yet he is only allowing a little in. The volunteers become part of his process of allowing.

And as they donate their time to help people like him, they are also inviting more energy into their lives. Their volunteer work is helping to create a stronger stream, a stronger flow in their own lives. It may create many other things, too – like gratitude for what they have, thankfulness that they have the time to help others, positive human interaction with other people as they volunteer, a feeling of usefulness and being of benefit – of service – to others.

Most people who participate in acts of generosity feel they receive more through their giving than the people they give to. They feel grateful for what their generosity brings them.

Donating time, kindness, stuff – whatever abundance you have – affirms prosperity in your life. It affirms that you have enough: so much that you can give some away.

Sharing what you have is a powerful statement of feeling prosperous. Yes, it is a wonderful, loving thing to do. But it can also help uplift you.

We often tell people who want to know how they can feel better, how they can increase their frequency: look for someone else to uplift. Look for someone else to help. Something as simple as sharing a smile can change a person's perspective on their day.

You have probably heard of the people who go through drive thru windows at coffee shops or restaurants, and pay for the order of the person behind them. Is the person in the vehicle behind them going to have a nice surprise? Yes. But the person who is paying for their order is going to get an even bigger boost.

Generosity gives back to the giver in many ways.

How many philanthropists work to earn even more so they have more money to give away? Many work well past the time when they could retire just to raise more funds to share, and to bring greater benefit to more lives.

Giving feels good.

Maybe you don't have a lot of money to give right now. But maybe you have a little extra time.

Maybe you don't have a lot of dollars to give, but you have a few. Giving away $1 or $5 feels better than not giving any when you want to.

Maybe you don't have time to donate, but you have some extra clothes in your closet you no longer wear, or items in your home that you don't use.

Maybe you can't give yet at the level you desire. But you can recognize what you are giving. Or find a way to donate an hour a week, a few hours a month.

You never want to give so that it feels like it is hurting you. Only give what you can freely give – what feels good to you to give.

So many people have skills and talents they can offer that will benefit someone else. Maybe they can teach. Or mentor. Or serve.

So many adults have a little extra time they could give to a child who is feeling alone and lonely, who believes no one cares. Or to animals that have been abandoned and need some loving attention.

Often, being generous means that you ask the cashier at the checkout about her day, and you *listen* to the response. You let the other person know that you actually see her, a fellow human being, and that you care.

It doesn't cost any money to be generous with kindness. And yet it can feel so good.

You have the ability to be generous today.

You have something that can uplift someone else today, and make that person's life a little brighter.

You have abundance to share.

Chapter 46: Too Much Stuff?

We know this chapter will not apply to everyone. Some people feel they have a shortage of stuff, and can't imagine ever having too much stuff.

Some people feel a shortage of money but a surplus of stuff. This chapter is for you.

Too much stuff creates a heaviness of energy. There is a feeling of excess heaviness, excess weight, items feeling burdensome. And these feelings can slow the flow of energy in your life – they can slow the flow of abundance.

A closet that is jammed full is not saying, "I have space for wonderful new things." It is resistant to new things. It is not inviting more. It is saying, "I have too much already."

Now, unless you have a "smart" closet, we know it is not really talking to you.

But your closet *is* talking to you *energetically*. Every time you look at it, you might admire the wonderful things it holds for you. Or you might be having other thoughts. And if it is not evoking positive thoughts and feelings from you, then you might want to consider making a change.

Maybe it is simply a matter of organizing your closet. Maybe it does not hold too much – it just stores items without organization.

But maybe there is a little – or lot – in there that you don't use anymore.

There was a best-selling book by author Marie Kondo on tidying that has inspired people to consider if the items in their spaces bring them joy. And if they don't spark joy,or serve a utilitarian purpose, then you thank them and re-home them.

People hold onto items for many reasons.

People who grew up with shortage might worry about shortage in their future, and feel they need to hold onto everything that comes their way for a possible future need.

Some people love to save money, and buy items they find on sale at great prices – even if they don't use them.

Some people attach emotion to items, or attach responsibility. For instance, they hold onto items that have been passed down to them by their parents or earlier generations. They don't feel they have the freedom to find new homes for these items. They feel a responsibility to care for them – even if caring for those items feels burdensome.

People hold onto clothes they don't wear that are no longer their size because they hope to be in that smaller size again. Or they worry they might gain weight back that they lost and be at that bigger size again. Or maybe the clothes evoke wonderful memories of a special event.

There are so many reasons people hold onto stuff. Someone gave you a gift that you can't stand, but you don't feel free to give it away. You put it on display for the two days every year this friend visits.

The first thing we want you to do is be amused with yourselves. (Because we find all of you, and your relationship with stuff, to be very amusing from non-physical.)

Don't beat yourself up for having too much stuff.

Don't beat yourself up for the reasons you have too much stuff.

Don't beat yourself up if you have too much stuff and don't feel inspired to lighten the amount of stuff in your life.

Make peace with where you are.

If you have lots of stuff and you are happy having lots of stuff, then you need to release any shame or guilt you might have about it. Lots of stuff is not nearly as much of a burden energetically if it doesn't evoke negative emotion from you. So hold onto your stuff if you can find a way to feel good about it – if you can let people into your home without shame or negative emotion. "This is me – I like a lot of stuff."

It is an issue when the stuff feels like too much – and it evokes negative emotion from you.

That is your signal you need to make a change.

What we would like you to consider is making incremental changes.

If you want to make big changes all at once – if you feel inspired to do that, find the time and energy to do that, and most of all, if that is pleasing to you – then wonderful. Follow your guidance.

What we find with most people is that little changes work better. Little changes start to change your frequency. And they are easier to do, one step at a time.

For instance, let's say you have six boxes of stuff in your basement. Yes, we know some of you have sixty or even six hundred.

Method 1

What we would encourage you to do is to take one box and sort through it. See if you can eliminate half of what is in the box –

recycling it or donating usable items to people or organizations who can use them. Or maybe you will even find something you can sell or consign.

What if you could get those six boxes down to three?

Energetically, that is a huge difference.

Maybe you decide to keep all of one box, but donate most of another box. Just see if there is a way to lighten up half the boxes.

Now, maybe half feels too strong. Do what you are comfortable with. Maybe you lighten the boxes by 25%, or 10%. Do what feels comfortable to you.

Method 2

If the first method feels too extreme, then consider having a Reconsider box. Take four sheets of paper. Label them *Recycle*, *Donate*, *Reconsider*, and *Keep*. Give them their own areas, or their own bags/boxes. These are your four piles where you will put items.

Go through the first box from your basement or attic. See if there are things you can place in the recycle and donate piles. And keep a trash container nearby in case there are items you must put there.

There will likely be some items you recognize you don't use and won't use but aren't quite ready to release yet. Put those in the "reconsider" pile. When you are through sorting, put these items into their own box, and label it "Reconsider." Then at a future point in time – three months, six months, a year – go back to this box. Sort through it again. You will likely be ready to release something in that box.

If you are sorting through a basement or attic full of boxes, you may have a whole stack of "reconsider" boxes. And that is okay. "Reconsider" means you are beginning the process of releasing attachment. It may just take a little while.

Over time, you might decide to move a few items from the "reconsider" pile back into the boxes you plan for now to keep indefinitely. But you might think about other items in those boxes and decide you are ready to release them.

You might think about items in your "reconsider" box or boxes and find people who can derive great benefit from them in the months ahead. You think of what is in that box and how happy or useful it might be to someone else. That makes it easier to give away.

Method 3

There are several ways this approach could be described. If going through a box or closet feels like too much commitment or work, then look for a single item to donate. Find something that you are not using, and know you probably won't use in the foreseeable future. Imagine someone else being really happy with this item. It brings them joy! You might give it to someone you know can use it, or give it to a charitable organization who will help it connect with its happy new owner.

Things enjoy being appreciated. Consider if the option is sitting at the back of a closet, forgotten, or getting worn by someone who is thrilled with it? Give the unneeded items in your home the opportunity to bring others joy, and to feel their happiness and appreciation.

You might decide to donate one item a day. Or seven a week. You might sort through boxes or closets once a month and pull out thirty items.

You know how much stuff you have that you want to lighten. And how much you feel comfortable donating/recycling. Maybe one item a week is huge progress for you.

If you can make this a habit, then over time, you will develop momentum.

Some people like to give away an item of clothing for every new one they bring home.

A new shirt comes home. An older shirt is given away. That is how they manage the size of their closets.

One in, one out.

Or, if you have an excess of items in your closet, it might be one in, two out.

You have the idea.

Get the Energy Moving Again

If the flow of energy around items in your home has been stagnant for a while, you need to get it moving again.

The feeling of too *much* stuff can slow down your receipt of prosperity.

A feeling that you have too much already, and that too much stuff is burdensome, is also saying energetically "no more."

You want to feel that energy is moving in your home, not that it is a place – or has places within it – that block the flow of energy.

You want your home – however big or small – to feel comfortable. To hold the things you need and that bring you joy and beauty – however you define beauty.

You want to step into your home and have it feel wonderful to you!

Old Beliefs?

Some of the reasons you hold onto unnecessary stuff may be tied to old beliefs.

If you trust that your non-physical support team is providing for you, and will help you connect with whatever you need when you need it, then you know whatever you need will come your way at the right time.

Since you have access to the unlimited resources of the Universe, you don't need to hold onto everything "just in case." Because you know if you might need something in the future, the Universe will find a way to bring it to you. It doesn't need to be that one in the box in your basement. The Universe will help match you up with one that is available through someone else – and that doesn't need to take up space in your home for years until it is needed again.

Moving from a shortage mentality to a mentality of abundance and accessibility means trusting that the Universe is going to make something available to you when you need it. This change doesn't happen overnight. But as you begin to trust in your own ability to create what you need, it will be easier to release what is not needed now. Because you know if you need it in the future, you will create it.

Trust your own internal guidance. Maybe you think about something you could give away, but then feel a tightness in your stomach, like your body is saying, "Not yet – hold onto it a little longer." And then you do need it shortly thereafter.

Non-physical looks at your energetic momentum, and knows what you will likely need in the near future. Non-physical will help guide you in what to release – and what not to. Trust your internal guidance – your intuition, your gut instinct. Non-physical is speaking to you...even about your stuff.

Chapter 47: An Environment of Success

You bring to any environment what you need to be successful. But why not create a physical environment that easily supports you?

You don't need a lot of space. But you need some space. You need some tools – whether that is a pen and paper, or access to a computer and phone.

Often, when people have been living with a mindset of shortage, they unintentionally create resistance in their physical environment, too. And what qualifies as "resistance" depends on you.

There are painters who love a messy studio – and painters who love cleanliness and organization, where every item they regularly use has a home, a space where it belongs between projects. There are writers and researchers who are so buried behind stacks of paper you have to look twice to find them at their desks. And there are others whose desks don't have a single piece of paper on top. Some gardeners like to throw seeds to the wind – literally, while others have a specific plan for where every seed is planted.

What is a successful environment for you?

Some people just want a box – *their* box. When the kids go to bed, they can pull out this box and quickly set out what they need to go to work – even if that "work" is meditation or yoga.

What kind of environment do you need to live in? To work in? To thrive in?

Some people like music in the background; others prefer silence. Some people can't work if there isn't a lot of human or animal activity around them. Others prefer to be alone.

What kind of space supports you feeling good? Not because you need it to feel good…because you never want how you feel to be conditional on your environment.

But because there are some environments where your body and soul sigh. They relax into their well-being and creativity thrives.

If you don't have that kind of space in your life, consider how you could begin to create it.

It can be small at first – a single item, a single box. Maybe a piece of paper you put on the wall with meaningful sayings. And then grow it. Grow the space that is supportive of you.

How do you define beauty – what uplifts you when you look at it? Maybe photographs of loved ones. Or fresh, fragrant flowers. Maybe an item you found somewhere that represents prosperity to you. Or you just feel good when you look at it.

Bring beauty into your environment.

Beauty is personal. It is a matter of individual taste. Some people like modern, crisp lines in black and white. Others want bright colors, floral prints. There are so many options, it doesn't make sense to list them. But you know beauty when you see it. You know what feels supportive of you. What you want to bring into your environment to look at every day, because looking at it uplifts you – it feels good.

Prosperity also means having beauty in your life. Having space that feels right to you. Having access to the tools you need. Feeling like your environment is supportive of you – and your success.

Take a moment and look at your environment. If looking at your space doesn't feel good, doesn't uplift you – think about how you can begin to transform it.

It doesn't take money to start. It just takes a sense of what you want and how you want to live.

It means one item. You start with one item, or a photograph of one beautiful item – that you can look at every day.

If money is short, you can start creating a visualization of your feel-good environment in your mind. Or on paper. As you focus on it and appreciate it every day, the Universe will start to bring you more to match it. And you will begin to see your physical space transform.

Find someplace you are living to call yours – your space of success, your space of beauty. Even if you are homeless, you can create the image in your mind. Or in a notebook you carry with you.

Give yourself the gift of spending time every day in an environment of beauty – indoors or out.

Allow yourself to have organization, however you define it. If you live in a cluttered home, you can create one corner of a table or desk or room or closet as a place to start. Just one little space that allows order into your environment. And by focusing on that every day, and appreciating it, you will notice organization growing in your life. If cleanliness is an issue for you, you can likewise start small, but bring it into your life somewhere. Appreciating even a little cleanliness every day will help it grow.

Often, your physical environment becomes a reflection of how you feel inside. It is an extension of your field of energy – and how you feel. For instance, if you feel a shortage of space for you in your life – a shortage of time for what matters most to you – you will likely see a manifestation of that in your environment. If you live with a busy family and it feels like your life revolves around the children, you might see the kids' stuff overtaking the house, and the house no longer reflecting you and the way you like to live.

Balance is crucial. A home should reflect all the personalities living there, and try to reflect a cooperative balance of the kinds of space that support each of them.

Having space that feels good to you is important. Maybe it is indoor space or outdoor space – or both. But consider what comes to mind when you think about living in an environment of success – an environment that feels good to you, supportive of you. What makes you smile as you arrive home and walk in the door? And then, as the saying goes, begin to "bring it home."

Chapter 48: Tug-of-War

Many of you are familiar with the rope game, Tug-of-War.

You take a very long, sturdy rope. In the center of the rope, a knot or piece of colored fabric is tied. Then two teams, of approximately the same strength and size, position themselves on each side of the rope, to pull against each other. The first team to pull the other team to their side wins.

When you have two teams that are equal in strength, the game can continue for a while. Teams that are uneven in strength will produce a very quick game. Each team is offering the other team resistance. The more resistance each team has, and the more balanced the resistance between the teams, the longer the game lasts.

Most of you envision your struggle with money like a tug-of-war game. Except you envision your opponent as the person you think is keeping you from winning. You might see your opponent as your parents, your spouse, your children, your employer. Your would-be-employer who won't give you that job yet. The rich relative who refuses to die. You might see your opponent as the government, a school or university, or the agency that won't give you the credentials to do what you want with your life.

We want you to understand that the only person you are challenging in a tug-of-war game is yourself.

You, and only you, are offering the resistance that is keeping you from winning what you want.

You have to leave everyone else out of it.

The pattern for many people is that you know what you want.

And then you think thoughts about why you can't have what you want, or how it will be hard to get.

Resistance.

You are providing your own resistance.

So you pull what you want a little closer.

And then your attention to resistant thoughts strengthens that feeling of "lack" and pulls you away from winning to that center point, to start all over again.

Some of you have been in a tug-of-war game with yourselves for years. Even decades.

You won't let yourself win.

You have thoughts that pull you toward what you want, and then thoughts which pull you away from what you want.

You can't get any momentum going.

The reason you might feel stuck is because the place where you are standing feels so familiar.

Because you keep pulling yourself back there.

If you sat in a car and slowly pushed the accelerator, then immediately the brake, then slowly the accelerator, then quickly the brake again – you wouldn't get very far. And certainly not very fast.

That is what a lot of you are doing with the energy of money.

You don't just apply the accelerator and move toward what you want. You brake. Apply the accelerator. Brake again.

You keep starting and stopping. Starting and stopping.

And then you wonder why you are frustrated, why you are so slow to make progress.

You are in an energetic battle...with yourself.

The empowering news is that you can stop providing yourself with opposition. You can stop offering yourself resistance on this topic.

You can decide you really do know where you want to go. And you are going to stop "braking" your own progress.

You can clean up your thoughts. You can get fussy about what you are thinking. Be particular.

Thoughts of resistance never feel good. So as soon as you find yourself having a resistant thought, just choose to stop it.

Stop it.

"Oh, that thought doesn't feel good. So it must be a resistant thought. Let me find a thought that feels a little better."

1) Focus on where you want to be.

2) Release thoughts that offer resistance to you getting there.

3) Replace those resistant thoughts with better feeling thoughts that allow you to continue your progress forward.

It sounds so simple. And it is!

But you have to be willing to let go of the resistance.

Some of you are so used to struggle that you are more comfortable there. Because struggle is familiar.

Easy success is not.

But it can be....

As soon as you begin to lessen the resistance you have been offering, you will notice progress. The progress may appear in little ways at first. But be attentive: you will notice a change.

And you might go: "Could it really have been this easy all the time? I just needed to get out of my own way?"

Yes.

You are the sole offerer of your vibration, of your point of attraction.

And you are the only one who can offer resistance.

If you continue to see someone else as holding power over you – if you continue to see them as offering resistance to what you want and the reason you can't get what you want – then you are, essentially, assigning them your own power. You can't give your power to them, in reality. But your perception of them as your resistance empowers the illusion of them having power over you. You always have the power.

Remember Dorothy's red shoes.

You always have the power, even if you aren't aware of it.

Chapter 49: Green Light Thoughts

Green thoughts? No, we aren't talking about the conservation movement or recycling.

When we talk about developing patterns of thought that move you to where you want to go in your life, and develop momentum in moving energy, it helps to have a simple analogy.

Traffic lights offer an easy comparison to the flow of energy that your thoughts generate. Because every thought generates energy. And that energy can offer progress or resistance toward what you desire, just like vehicles at stop lights.

Consider a green light as an allowing thought. It lets you move forward, toward where you want to go. It is in alignment with what you want.

A red light is resistance. It keeps you from making progress toward what you desire.

Are your thoughts about what you want green lights or red lights?

Ask yourself: "Is this thought green or red? I am moving toward what I want with green. I am not making progress with red."

Maybe your thoughts are more like the yellow traffic light. Often with yellow thoughts, you feel a sense of caution.

Yellow provides warning. Strong resistance ahead. Red light soon.

Red thoughts, green thoughts, yellow thoughts?

You may not have control over the traffic signals, although they can be cooperative components.

You do have control over your thoughts and over the topics where you direct your focus. Choose your thoughts the same way! Choose green light thoughts aligned with progress in reaching what you desire.

Chapter 50: Affirmations of Habit

People don't stop to consider that their activities – particularly activities in which they engage frequently, or even daily – are presenting and affirming where they now stand in relationship to prosperity. You have developed habits for a reason. You engage in these activities daily. And these activities all have a vibration that they reflect – one you are offering. Sometimes, these habits are affirming where you now stand financially – even if you are not aware of it. And they become affirmations that continue to affirm where you are, not necessarily where you want to be.

Take, for instance, the purchase of a cup of coffee. Some people buy a small because they think a larger size is too expensive, or doesn't fit in their budget. Some don't get the drink they want because they don't have the money. Some order water in a restaurant to save the money that a beverage would cost. For some, being frugal is part of demonstrating that you do value money. But for others, it is sending a message that "I don't have enough."

What is the energetic frequency – and the emotion – behind some of your regular habits?

Going to a grocery store, consider what thoughts you are having as you make purchases. How much is the cost of an item playing a role in what you purchase? And more importantly, what are the emotions that accompany a purchase?

For instance, let's say you take your son to the grocery store. He wants to buy the brand-name cookies, and you tell him, "No, we will get this store brand because they are on sale." Or, "I know you like those better, but these are cheaper." Is the feeling you are conveying that you value saving money, and therefore don't want to spend more? Or that you don't have enough money to get what he wants, so he needs to settle for something less desirable? If he is not feeling good about what you are saying, you are also likely not feeling good telling him. If you are in alignment with what you mean, and you can help him to align too, then it will be a more positive experience for both of you.

As you go through your daily routine, consider what messages you are affirming. Are you feeling appreciative of what you do have? Are you disliking your situation and feeling that you can't afford what you want?

Clothing is another example. Many people love finding bargains, no matter how much money they have. Others feel their clothes are inferior to co-workers or friends because they can't afford more, and don't feel as good about what they are wearing. Some people like to brag about how little they paid for a great outfit. While others don't want to share what they paid because they feel ashamed they can't afford better, or they don't want to mention where they bought it. Two people could wear exactly the same attire, yet one is thrilled and the other is embarrassed. One loves to shop at a thrift store to save money and get great value. Another is embarrassed because that is the only store where she can afford to shop.

Going to the movies, some will only go at the discount hours – like weekday afternoons – because they don't want to spend more. While others go in the afternoon because they don't feel they can afford to pay full-price in the evenings.

At restaurants, do you look at the prices on the menu first? Or do you figure out what you want, and then consider price – or not consider price at all?

Do you shop with coupons because you enjoy saving money, or does it feel like you can't afford to pay full price and get what you want? Some people love the thrill of a bargain, or saving as much as they can off full retail price. Others feel like they "have to" shop with coupons – and may feel burdened by the time and energy *they spend* to save a few dollars.

These situations are all very individual, and will vary tremendously according to the person and his or her values. All we want to do is to make you aware that you may have thoughts and feelings you are offering about activities in which you engage regularly – that are affirming a feeling of prosperity, or lack of it.

Begin to bring greater awareness to these activities. If you find any thoughts and feelings which seem negative, work with them to shift the frequency higher.

We are not encouraging you to change habits that you can't afford to change, or don't want to. We are encouraging you to uncover and bring to light what you are affirming in your life on a daily basis.

Routine activities often have routine thoughts that accompany them. And those thoughts and subsequent feelings are broadcasting certain messages to the Universe. Work to align your thoughts with positive frequencies. Lay tracks on purpose. Daily habits mean daily affirmations. Be sure yours align with where you want to be. Be sure you are enjoying green light thoughts that let you move freely toward your intended destination.

Chapter 51: Monetary Karma

Sometimes we encounter people who believe they are suffering monetarily in their lives because of karma. They believe they did something in a past life that they are now paying for – literally. Maybe they were wealthy in a previous life and didn't treat others well. Maybe they stole from someone so think their current poverty is retribution. Maybe they believe they chose to be poor in this life so they could learn to be sensitive to the needs of others less fortunate. There are all sorts of reasons that people make up – or have been told by others – as to why they are not enjoying prosperity now.

And we want to say to you, in the kindest and most loving of ways, that you did nothing in your past – this life or a previous life – that is keeping you from being successful financially. *Unless you believe it is so.*

Karma is a greatly misunderstood spiritual concept. So let's correct it. First of all, each physical life experience is new and fresh. You don't drag punishment or retribution into this life because of something you did in a previous physical experience. Considering how many lives you have had before this one, you would all be dragging lots of baggage around with you from one life to the next. That is simply not the way karma works.

You have all committed wonderful loving acts in your earlier lives – and you have all done and experienced things which you would choose not to repeat. So each life, you begin anew. There is no karmic lesson or retribution for which you are now paying.

But if you believe there is, then you will create that experience in response to your belief. If you believe you did something wrong in the past and you are paying for it now, then you will create a life that is a match to that frequency. So if you believe a lack of prosperity is payment for "sins of the past," so to speak, we encourage you to release that false belief. It is not so.

You understand the law of attraction. You attract back to you what is a match to the frequency you are offering. That's karma, plain and simple. In this life. This same life. Sometimes in the same minutes, the same day, the same week. Law of attraction can work quickly when there is no resistance. Little stuff with no resistance often happens faster than the bigger stuff – however you define that for yourself.

We choose not to use the word karma, generally speaking, because it is one of the most abused and misunderstood spiritual concepts that abounds.

You are the creator of your life experience.

Karma implies judgment that some more powerful being is placing on you. And since all the "powerful" non-physical beings in the Universe love and adore you, they would never want you to suffer. It is simply not logical.

What you offer, energetically, is what you attract back to you. Like frequencies attract. Karma is the name for what is a match to what you are offering – to the energy that you are bringing to your very own self.

You create your own karma. You are doing it this very minute.

Since you are the sole offerer of your vibration, if you don't like what you are attracting, you can change it.

You have the power to change your own karma. And you can begin changing it immediately.

So let the past go. Focus on where you want to be. And start heading there now.

Allow your "good karma" to catch up with you.

Chapter 52: Creator, Entrepreneur

Some qualities of an entrepreneur:

– creative thinker

– exercises initiative

– benefits from an opportunity

– a decision maker

– personally invested in the venture

– assesses indicators of success.

We see all of you as entrepreneurs. And we think you would benefit from seeing yourself that way, too.

You are all creators of your life experience. There may be others you allow to influence you. But ultimately, you are responsible for your own life. (Which also means you have the power to change it.)

If you see yourself as an entrepreneur, we think it would allow your thinking to expand. You are the entrepreneur of your venture in this life—whatever that venture is. Many of you are also entrepreneurs of businesses.

Many of the same values are required in both, whether you are talking about your life or your business. They are your creations, and you are the energetic force driving them.

Self-identified entrepreneurs often talk about passion. They love what they do. They care deeply about it. We want you to care deeply about your lives. We want you to feel passionately.

Entrepreneurs find fulfillment in their work. It often doesn't feel like work because it is meaningful to them. We want you to find fulfillment in your lives. We want you to enjoy people and activities that are meaningful.

We want you to understand that you are a powerful creator – far more powerful than you have probably allowed yourself in the past to believe. You are powerful. You are a creator.

You have the resources of the entire Universe available to you. There is no shortage – unless you believe there is. The Universe, and a whole support team in non-physical, is lined up to assist you, and to help you be successful.

You demonstrate initiative every single day. From the time you wake up, you are assessing, taking action, getting things done.

You see opportunities and know they are being presented to you for a reason: you attracted them. You decide if they are opportunities you want to align yourself with, that will bring benefit to you.

You make decisions, solve problems, apply common sense to find solutions and next steps. You are a decision maker.

This is your life. Of course you are invested in it personally! Of course you want it to be everything you are hoping for.

You know how you are looking at your life. Are you seeing your own success? Or are you refusing to see what you do that is "right" and moving you forward – and everything is "right" because it is all moving you forward.

You can assess your own feelings. You know what feels good and what doesn't. You know, often before it even happens, how things will turn out because of how they feel to you.

You get to define what success is to you. Happiness? Satisfaction? Fulfillment?

What brings meaning to your life? Relationships? Family? Time well-spent? Financial success is not a measurement of you as a person. Money alone doesn't bring joy. We're not saying it isn't fun and rewarding to bring more abundance into your life. We are saying that money alone doesn't bring fulfillment and joy. There are very wealthy people who are unhappy because they were lead into believing that money was enough. It's not.

Many people lead very successful lives yet money plays a small role in their lives. History and family genealogies are full of stories of people who made major contributions to improve the lives of those around them, yet had little or no money. Many of those are people we would consider to be very successful at creating lives that mattered. They were in alignment with who they were and with what they wanted.

So, dear entrepreneur, consider how you want the venture that is your life to move forward. How will you assess your own future success?

You are like someone who is starting a new business. You have ideas about what you want your life to be, how you want to see it expand and grow. You can create a vision, align with manifesting that vision, then take inspired action to bring it to fruition.

Your life is your business – in more ways than one!

We see you as successful, and we know you can be successful in the ways that are most meaningful to you.

Isn't it time you see yourself that way?

Chapter 53: The Power of Focus

Imagine that you want to visit San Francisco. And you live far away. Maybe you live in the Midwest, or the eastern United States. You have decided to drive to San Francisco.

Consider these three scenarios.

In the first one, you are focused on getting to San Francisco as soon as you can. You get in your car and you drive. You stop as safety requires, for food, gas, and just enough sleep so you can keep going. You stay focused on getting there, and getting there quickly.

In the second scenario, you are focused on getting to San Francisco. But you also want to enjoy the journey. So you start off driving, but make stops along the way at interesting sites, good restaurants, beautiful vistas. You meet interesting people. You have fun with the journey. It takes longer to get to San Francisco, but the trip itself has been enjoyable, memorable, and fun.

In the third scenario, you get in your car and start for San Francisco. San Francisco is your destination. But along the way, you have so much fun! You take your time, and are enjoying the journey so much that San Francisco becomes less meaningful to you. You wander and explore. You make amazing discoveries of places and people you never knew existed. Along the way, your priorities change. Maybe there is a new lover, or a new passion. A place that feels like home. Maybe there is a new dog or cat or child. A job you adore. You choose to shift your priorities. Your original destination of San Francisco leads you to what feels like a much better, happier one. San Francisco may – or may not – remain a dream destination for "someday." But you are happy where you are now, and that feels like it is all that matters. The choice of your original destination – San Francisco – made all of this possible, whether you get there or not.

The original point of focus for all of these scenarios was San Francisco. In the first two, San Francisco was reached, but with very different journeys, very different experiences of getting there. In the second scenario, there were many points of focus while still achieving the larger priority. In the third scenario, San Francisco was the original priority, but new priorities emerged along the way. New points of meaningful focus were established.

When there is something you want – someplace you want to go in your life, something you want to achieve – you get to choose the "getting there." You also get to choose different paths along the way. You can even change your priorities totally and decide to go somewhere else. The journey is yours.

Most of you have experienced talking to a child or young person who is very involved in something they are doing – maybe reading a book or playing a game. They are strongly immersed in the frequency of what they are enjoying. They are focusing. Concentrating. And then you, grownup, come along with a different priority, on a totally different frequency. And they don't hear you. They don't see you. You are non-existent to them in that moment. Which grownups usually find frustrating. And the kids find it annoying that you are interrupting them and their bliss in what they are enjoying. You are in your own, very different, vibrational worlds. Very different frequencies. It is not that one is right and one is wrong. They are just not compatible, or synchronistic, frequencies in that moment.

Focus has incredible power. You are flowing energy through you in a particular direction, toward the object of your attention. And the power of your energy flow is also activating the law of attraction, bringing you more to match the frequency you are holding.

You have to remember that the Universe expects that you choose the objects of your attention. And since you have free will – you can pay attention to anything – then the Universe figures you are giving it your attention because you like it and want more of it. So with the law of attraction, you will attract more to you of where you are directing your focus. You will bring more to you that is a vibrational match.

When you activate the subject of money, are you activating its presence or its absence? Anything you want in your life – and don't have – invites you to consider: what frequency am I really activating when I focus on this topic? And all you have to do is look around, because what you are living is the evidence of what you are activating.

Do keep in mind, however, the power of momentum. If you have recently started to activate a new, higher frequency, it may take some time for you to build momentum on that frequency. And for that momentum to gain power, and power in its point of attraction. So if you feel you are building momentum on a new frequency, continue to celebrate your progress and build it! Don't give up because you aren't in San Francisco yet, if that is still your destination. Just continue to re-direct your focus toward what you want.

Many people can imagine what it is like to be in a new place – like San Francisco – even if they have never been there. It is the desire to be there and fully experience it that feeds the focus and choosing of that place as a destination. Let's face it – you wouldn't choose a place to go that you don't want to experience. You must want the experience of being there, and believe it will hold positive value for you.

You need to resonate with what you want.

Many of you have been resonating with the lack of something you want, not the having of it.

Or you focus on the having of things you don't want, like bills and expenses and taxes, instead of on the enoughness or abundance of money to easily pay them.

Let's imagine you are starting a new business. You are very focused on the creation of the new business. You are excited and having fun with the many aspects of opening a new business.

And then you open it. And at first it is fabulous. But there are also now many more details demanding your attention. There are new concerns, like pleasing customers. There are more bills to pay. You become more aware of what fellow business owners tell you, and all the trials and tribulations of their past experiences that they share. You start thinking about how much money you are taking in – and worry if it is enough. Your focus shifts from San Francisco, and enjoying your thriving business, to the hot pavement and where is the next gas station and why is the gas much more expensive here, and yes, you are hungry but not sure if you want to try that odd-looking restaurant even though you haven't seen another one in a long time. And now your phone isn't picking up a signal.

And you aren't picking up a signal either – at least one you like. You have tuned from what you want to what can be worried about, to what is not desired. You have shifted your focus. Yes, you do still have a focus, and you are still in control of it (even though it might not feel like you are in control of it anymore). But the car isn't going toward San Francisco very quickly now. The focus has shifted, and so has your temporary destination.

In sports, you learn that the ball is going to follow your vision when you throw it. You need to look at where you want it to end up before you throw it. You have to focus on the destination, the target. Clarity about your destination means increased likelihood that the ball will reach it.

Life is like that, too.

In baseball and softball, a successful pitcher doesn't think about where the ball could end up before throwing it. Because there are many more unwanted destinations for that ball than wanted. A pitcher focuses and decides the ball's intended destination before releasing it. Considering where the pitcher doesn't want the ball to go clutters the desired frequency. Where does the pitcher want the ball to go?

There is clarity in focus. There is clarity in intention. Put the two together – focused intention, intentional focus – and you have a powerful combination.

Add to that focus the momentum of what works. What you know works. What has worked before. What you believe – and expect – to work again.

If there is a subject in your life you focus on, and your experience with that subject is negative, then you probably want to focus as little there as possible. Because you are building momentum on that topic as unsuccessful, as not working.

But if you had even one experience with that topic that did work, you can think about that one experience over and over again until you associate that topic with success.

Think about where you intend your life to be. Focus there. Focus on the destination you are intending your ball to reach.

Then open for guidance and inspiration. And allow the law of attraction to do its work.

Chapter 54: The Power of Allowing

When a pitcher throws the ball toward its intended destination, the pitcher lets the ball go. Releases it.

The pitcher has infused energy into the throw, and made clear the intention about where the ball is to end up.

But the pitcher does not follow the ball every inch of the way to home plate. Maybe visually. But not physically.

The pitcher needs to allow the ball to do its work. To reach its destination.

Can it be thrown off course? Can it land somewhere other than its intended target?

Just imagine how boring the game of baseball would be if every pitcher struck out every batter. There would be no reason to play the game. No one would go. It wouldn't be interesting. Not if every pitcher's ball landed exactly where the pitcher intended.

When you plant a seed in the ground, you don't dig it up constantly to see if it is growing. You have to allow it time to grow, to mature. You must allow the seed time for its own growth and expansion.

Does allowing the seed the time it needs also mean it will definitely become the plant you are hoping for? Of course not. But if you keep digging the seed up to check on its progress, and are watching it constantly, it can not grow.

There is power in allowing.

A lot of people think allowing is lazy. It's not.

It's kind of like parenting, when you see your child have an opportunity to do the "right thing," maybe the kind thing. You have to stand back and see what your child does. You might have all your fingers crossed. But you know your child needs an opportunity to be kind without being prompted by you. You need to allow your child the chance to make a choice from his or her own internal guidance.

And if the child makes a different choice from what you are hoping, that's okay. The child is learning. Sometimes children learn more from their mistakes than from times they get it "right."

When you ask for something from the Universe, from Source, from your non-physical support team – you need to allow time for an answer. You need to let go of the pitch.

The "ask" was the pitch, the planting of the seed.

How do you know if you are allowing the seed to grow?

Your emotions let you know.

If you feel good about the seed growing, and you are truly expectant of positive results, then you are allowing.

If you are skeptical or doubtful or even pessimistic that the seed is growing, and you are not feeling good when you think about it, then you are offering resistance.

Your emotions are your first indicator.

Can you enjoy knowing the seed is growing, even if you aren't watching it physically manifest into what you want?

Remember that everything is energy first. Is thought first.

You can *feel it* into being. You can tell it is growing – without digging it up – because of how you feel.

Imagine that you are standing outdoors in the dark. And you are wondering how to get home.

Imagine that you are on a very clear path that will lead you home if you just follow it.

Except it is dark. You don't see the path. You don't even realize you are standing on the path to where you want to go.

The path is right beneath you, where you are standing.

But you don't know it.

Allowing means that you let the path light up.

You don't make it light up.

You just allow your eyes to adjust, and let your vision tune to what is there – not to what isn't.

And as you patiently allow your vision to adjust to the darkness, you discover that you are standing on the path to what you want.

It was there all along. You were on the path all along. You just didn't know it.

You allowed yourself to open, to receive, to see.

You want to be easy about this process of manifestation. You want to trust yourself – and what you are creating vibrationally. You need to be able to trust your own vibration, and expect that you are creating the good things you want in your life.

As you stand there and adjust to this place of allowing, thoughts and ideas begin coming to you. The resources and contacts come to you. You are attracting to you just what you need to create what you want in your life.

Imagination, inspiration, and intuition are all part of the unfolding.

Allowing means that you are letting the law of attraction work, instead of using effort attempting to force what you want into place.

When there is a lot of resistance being offered, people often try to make something happen. And it takes an awful lot of effort to try and overcome resistance.

It is much easier to tune your frequency to what is wanted, then allow the magic to begin. We say magic because that is often how it feels – like everything starts coming to you easily. It is actually the laws of the Universe at work. Except now you are working with them – and allowing them to do their work – instead of trying to overcome resistant momentum and force something into place.

Have you ever tried to open a jar, and no matter how hard you tried to twist that jar lid, you just couldn't get it open? And then you hand the jar to someone else, and they easily open it?

Frustrating, right? And funny!

You expected it not to work. And the more you engaged in resistance with the jar lid, the more it seemed like it was intentionally fighting you.

And then someone else, in a place of allowing, took the jar, and it just seemed to open so easily! That person was not offering resistance, frustration, tons of effort. They just let it happen. They *allowed* it. And energy that is offered without resistance is powerful.

If you are not experiencing something you want in your life – if you are not allowing abundance to come to you – then it can only be that you are offering resistance and not allowing it. You just need to tune your frequency higher.

Be easy about it. Allowing is not something you make happen, or force. It is throwing the pitch and releasing it.

If you don't release the pitch, it can never reach its intended destination.

Your vibration does the work.

Allow the ball to reach home.

Chapter 55: The Power of Alignment

Have you seen a group of ducklings follow a parent around a pond or lake? They tend to waddle after the parent, forming a single line. It is an alignment of ducks: ducklings on parade.

When there is something you want, we would like you to think about your thoughts like those ducklings. You have your parent thought – your desire. Allow the rest of your thoughts to be thoughts that line up with that original desire. They all move together toward a single destination. Thoughts on parade.

The parent duck is not making those ducklings get in line. It simply happens. They are all enjoying a singular vibration. The parent leads and the ducklings align with following.

Your thoughts can be a little more complicated. Mostly because you are out of practice with allowing alignment. On some topics, your thoughts are not parades at all, but more random. They dart here, then there, then way over there. It you were a spectator in the grandstands observing this chaos, it might be amusing to watch. But when you are living it, the results are not so entertaining.

The ducklings intuitively follow the parent. But they also intuitively know they just need to follow the duckling ahead of them. Because they all want to be happy; they all have similar desires.

So Duckling A doesn't have to ask Duckling B: where are you going? Because Duckling A knows Duckling B also wants to go where it feels good.

This may seem like a silly analogy to you. But we want you to understand that those ducklings understand alignment. They understand, on an instinctive level, what it feels like to be part of a group that has momentum in movement forward.

Manifestation involves thought first, then more thoughts in alignment with your original desire. As more thoughts line up, momentum builds. And the power of attraction also builds, attracting more thoughts at like frequencies.

You are the parent duck.

And you want your thoughts to be in alignment, not chaos.

Alignment is the natural state of being, so it is about *allowing* alignment.

Which really means: getting out of your own way.

Having positive thoughts.

Having general positive thoughts, until enough positive momentum is established.

Having thoughts which allow the infinite supply of resources and well-being to flow to you.

Alignment

There are really two kinds of alignment. There is alignment with what you want. And there is alignment with Source.

The most powerful, most fun alignment is when you are in alignment with Source and with what you want. It is a singular alignment.

That is true power. That is when you feel the energies of the Universe moving through you in the most exciting of ways.

That is joyful alignment. Passion. Ecstasy. Exaltation. Bliss.

Fun!

Those are the kind of moments you came here to experience.

Ah, yes, the other stuff too.

But there is no greater feeling than true alignment with who you are and what you want – alignment with Source, and with the Source within.

So now you might ask, "How do I get there? It sounds great. But how do I get there?"

A little bit at a time.

If you have been practicing thought chaos – if you have not been picky about how you feel – then it is going to take a while to get your thoughts in alignment. And to allow that to become your practiced, natural-feeling state, instead of random reaction to whatever comes to mind or appears in front of you.

We aren't kidding about this. We want you to choose to feel good. And to choose thoughts that feel good to think about.

Do you know how different your lives would be if your own happiness really mattered to you?

A lot of you tell us you are practicing self-love. But if you really loved yourself, you wouldn't let yourself feel bad.

You wouldn't click on your computers and phones on news stories with sensational headlines that you know are not going to bring you good feelings.

You would be picky about where you direct your attention.

Your mind is going to expand the frequency of wherever you are directing your attention. So be really fussy about where you direct your thoughts.

"Is this news story going to generate positive feelings in alignment with where I want to go?"

Then don't listen to it. Don't read it.

At the beginning, it can feel like you are making lots of choices – maybe new choices.

But over time, momentum builds. Feeling good becomes a habit. And you are no longer tempted to click on those stories because they aren't part of the momentum you have been building. You know they don't belong in your parade.

So, in terms of this book, and your desire to increase your prosperity, think about your parade of thoughts. Your prosperity parade.

Are your thoughts in alignment with the having of what you want?

Do these thoughts fit, or not? If they don't fit, then just remove your attention.

The thoughts that don't fit in will wander off, all on their own, once you have enough momentum established. They aren't a vibrational match to your parade.

And the stronger the momentum of your parade builds, the more you will attract new thoughts that align with your desire, with your forward movement.

No more chaos.

As you find greater alignment, and your thinking aligns with the prosperity you desire, you will find more and more good things flowing to you. More ideas. More inspiration. More connections. More resources.

It will all unfold easily. Because you are in alignment, and you are letting law of attraction do its work.

Chapter 56: The Power of Prosperity

Have you ever watched a superhero movie or television show that showed the character discovering his or her own superpower? Learning how to use it?

It is important for you to claim your own prosperity power. Because the power already belongs to you. If you haven't realized it before, we hope you do now.

You have the ability to create – to attract, to allow – prosperity into your own life. The energy of prosperity is already flowing to you.

Claim it.

It is yours. It has been yours all along. You were born with it.

This dynamic energy is already flowing to you.

So is guidance from non-physical full of creative ideas and inspiration about how to align with financial abundance.

Now, it may not come all at once. But you can begin to step up a little higher vibrationally, allowing a little more abundance into your life. A little more inspiration.

And then step up again, a little higher.

And a little higher.

As you climb the stairs to a more prosperous life, your emotions will feel better and better.

You will feel more empowered.

You will feel more like you are living a life as the magnificent being that you truly are.

And the better you feel, the more you are aligning with who you really are, and with the life you came here to live.

Feel your way to joy. To happiness. To fulfillment. To alignment with Source.

And as you feel better and better, you will attract greater abundance into your life.

Feel your empowerment.

Feel your inspiration.

Feel your joy.

Feel who you really are...and let your brilliance shine.

Remember that feeling better *is* manifestation.

Feeling good *really matters*.

And if you are someone who has become tolerant of not feeling good, tolerant of negative emotions, tolerant of not having enough...

Stop it!

Because that is not your work. That is not who you are, or the life you came here to live.

And you know that. You can feel the "offness" of it.

Joyful expansion is not about settling for less.

It is about reaching forward, outward.

Joyful expansion is natural to you,

just as feeling prosperous is natural to you.

And if you have been temporarily separated from it,

that's okay. Because you have the power to change it.

You can start living your life as the amazing being you really are.

You can start allowing more prosperity into your life.

You can start telling yourself, "I have a right to feel good. It doesn't matter what is going on with the people around me, the world around me. I don't need anyone else to feel good in order for me to feel good. How they feel is their business. Circumstances don't have to affect me the way they have in the past. Because I am in charge of my own happiness. I am in charge of feeling good. I am going to spend more time every day looking for reasons to feel good. Finding things to appreciate. Finding things to do that fulfill me. I am going to stop settling for less than the life I know I came here to live."

It can feel audacious to claim your power of prosperity.

And that's okay.

It's not audacious at all.

Because this flow of energy came with you at birth.

It belongs to you.

It has always belonged to you.

Maybe you got temporarily separated from allowing it to flow fully. But you can change that now.

You can choose, in this moment, to start feeling good,

to be fussy about how you feel, and where you direct your attention;

to choose thoughts that feel in alignment with who you really are. Thoughts that are in alignment with Source and how Source sees you. Thoughts that are in alignment with what you really know, inside, to be true *about you*.

That you are worthy of audacious prosperity.

That you are worthy of a happy and fulfilling life.

That you deserve to feel good every day, no matter what.

And no matter what you are living, you can choose thoughts every day that allow the well-being, that bring you joy to think about – thoughts that feel good to you.

Because you are worthy of feeling good every single day of your life.

You deserve it.

Chapter 57: Prosperity Mindset

Even though we have been talking about abundance in this book, we have not talked much about wealth – yet.

Not using that specific word.

Because if you are struggling to get to the frequency of *enough*, then a word like *wealth* can feel very far away.

Now, we know many of you are already well beyond *enough*, and are reaching higher still.

Which is great.

So if it feels comfortable, we encourage you to try to find people who already have a prosperity mindset, and see what you can learn from them.

See how they talk about the world. How they are in the world.

How they live in the world.

Listen to the language they use. Look at their non-verbal communication.

We aren't talking about how they dress, or what jewelry or sunglasses they wear.

How do they think? Do they think differently than you do?

Do they relate to the world differently?

Most of these people were relating to the world differently before the money came...and that's why the money came.

There may be habits of thought...and action...that are similar to you. Or different than you.

And that can be interesting to find out.

It doesn't mean that you want to copy them, or emulate them, or place them on a pedestal.

It does mean you might consider your own habits of wealth…whatever those are.

Most millionaires make their own bed in the morning.

Many billionaires and millionaires pick up trash on the sidewalk outside their businesses…because they care. They don't want trash outside the front door to be someone's first impression of their business.

Many will stop to pick up a coin that has been dropped on the sidewalk – because every cent counts.

There are many habits that successful people have, that often run contrary to what people expect.

What are your habits of success?

Likewise, it is good to learn about money – if you haven't already. Because it is not just about accumulating wealth, but also managing it. Growing it.

People with lots of assets know how to manage their own money. They know how to invest. Managing money is a part of their lives – they don't just hire other people to do it. If you care about money, then you care about continuing to have money.

Most successful people are philanthropists. They give to charities that matter to them.

Even if you don't have the funds to invest right now, you can start attending free seminars and classes to learn how to think differently – better – about money.

You can watch free videos online. You can read books.

You can use your intuition to guide you to places where you can learn more about money – having it, saving it, investing it, managing it, growing it, giving it away.

Many people who grow up with wealth are used to learning about money in this way – used to thinking about money from a broader perspective. If you are not wealthy (yet), then start educating yourself so that you are ready as the abundance arrives.

There are lots of people who think, *I don't need to learn about money because I don't have it yet.*

But when you do have it, is that the time to *begin* learning?

See how it feels to learn about money. Do you find it interesting? Exciting?

Or do you end up feeling worse about yourself because you are comparing yourself to the situations of others who have more dollars *right now*, instead of looking toward your future?

Remember: do what feels good to you. Direct your focus.

Maybe you want to get to "enough" or "more than enough" before you start this process.

But at least you are integrating it into your horizon.

Maybe you already have a graduate degree in business or finance. But have you been considering how you would like to manage your own money, or just the money of others?

There is no right or wrong here. But learn about money. And have fun doing it!

We know we are being a bit vague in this chapter. But our wonderful readers are at very different points in your lives and your prosperity journeys.

It may be helpful to consider your financial objectives. What money does it feel realistic for you to reach for...this coming year? Next year?

Think about where you want to be standing financially in five years, ten years...twenty.

It's important to look beyond where you are standing right now, in this present moment.

Don't reach so big that it feels unattainable. But do allow your mind to wander...and have fun.

What is your vision of where you want to be? How would you describe your vision – succinctly and enthusiastically – using feeling words? How does your vision feel?

In strategic planning exercises, organizations often select their key values. If you were to define three or four values that represent who you are, and how you live in the world, what words would you choose? What values are most important to you?

Now think about the vision you have of your financial future. Do your vision and core values align?

Abundance often increases gradually. So you do have time. But if you want more abundance in your life, it can be helpful to prepare for its coming. Begin the process of learning about having money.

People who feel a lack of current financial resources don't often look much beyond the next paycheck or hoped-for income. They are trying to figure out how to pay the bills and stay financially afloat.

The challenge is, as long as you are staying so focused on the present, you are not looking at where you are going, and where you want to go.

You are not expanding your horizon to include your long-term future.

When many people think about abundance, they think about how they want to spend money: about the outflow of energy. They don't spend as much, or more time and attention, on the inflow of money, or on the flow of money while it is in their lives. It can be a lot of fun to think about *bringing* money into your life – not just spending it. Consider creating a balance of energy – of flow.

Open doors to learn more from those who have prosperity now. Open your mind to consider your potential income, and to allow ideas about ways to attract greater prosperity into your life.

If you didn't grow up with wealth, then educating yourself will help you to start learning the language of money. And it will broaden the way you think about financial abundance...beyond enough to pay the bills. It will help to expand your horizon...and your frequency. Expanding your mindset can expand your world.

Chapter 58: Appreciation and Gratitude

You have probably already heard about the power of gratitude, and how many people recommend gratitude as a way of living. But it is also important to understand the role of gratitude in affirming what you *already* have.

When you are grateful for what is in your experience already, you are saying to the Universe: *It is here and I value it. Thank you.*

One of the biggest powers of gratitude is that it affirms what you have – what you have for which you are feeling thankful. And as you are thankful for the presence of something in your life, you are offering a vibration for something that is there. You are already experiencing the physical manifestation of it, the feeling of it.

Gratitude is like thanking the Universe, Source, for a gift. You are acknowledging something you received. You are affirming the presence of it in your life, not the absence of it.

It has already manifested.

Gratitude is a powerful affirmation. And when you affirm the presence of something desired in your life, your vibrational frequency is inviting more to come to you that matches that frequency. Because – we want you to really understand this – you are affirming the presence of something desired. The creative process is not just energetically done. It is physically manifested. You created it.

So be thankful, of course. But also realize that gratitude is an affirmation.

The challenge is that sometimes, people drag an emotional vibration of unnecessary "baggage" into gratitude. It muddles the wanted with the unwanted. For instance, "Thank you FOR FINALLY sending this." It might be a feeling of desperation, or relief. It may be something you wanted or needed for a long time, and there is a sense "I never thought I would ever get it." Or "I never thought I would have it again."

So the act of being thankful can be clouded with feelings that don't enhance it. If you are thankful for something you worked really hard for, it may be a feeling that you have to work really hard to earn something to be grateful for. Or that you must have done something right – at last – to have been worthy of receiving what you wanted for so long.

Appreciating something can be "cleaner" vibrationally, because people don't tend to drag any sense of absence into it. Or how hard they had to work for it. Or how long it was in coming.

Appreciation is seeing the value in something now, and feeling it. Finding the positive aspects of anyone or anything. It is more pure to the present moment.

You can go on a walk and find things to appreciate.

You can sit in a room or vehicle and find things to appreciate.

You can simply *think* about people or experiences in your life that you value, and feel the warmth and gladness that they are there.

Many people interchange the words *gratitude* and *appreciation*. And there is nothing wrong with that. But it is important to understand what vibration you are really offering.

Because, with law of attraction, you will attract more to feel that way about.

So practice gratitude. But clarify what the feeling means to you. And clean it up, if necessary.

Be thankful for what you create in your life. For what you attract in your life. Because they are all indicators of the frequencies you are offering. They are all great feedback.

Appreciate often. All the time. Every chance you have.

Imagine that you give a gift to someone. They open it, and they absolutely adore the gift. They are thrilled and delighted. Compliments about this amazing present flow easily from them. They are so very pleased and happy.

Do you need them actually to say *thank you* in order for you to feel that your gift was appreciated? Of course not. You can tell how much the gift means to them. You can feel from them how much they love it.

Someone else might open a gift and say thank you right away. They expressed their gratitude. But you're disappointed in their reaction. You just don't feel the gift had as much significance for them as you had hoped.

It's not the words. It's the frequency. It's the feeling.

Chapter 59: Flow

So, now you are more ready than ever to allow greater abundance into your life. To notice what is already there and to appreciate it. To shift your thinking and feeling to a higher frequency, again and again.

As we noted early on, the flow of abundance – of all you need, and more – is natural. It is part of your birthright. It is who you are, at your core. It is the essence of you.

It is not about working ten times harder than you are now (which is impossible, anyway). It is about leveraging the power of energy alignment to work smarter. And to work in alignment with what you want to accomplish, what desires you want to manifest.

Allowing greater ease into your life also means allowing inspiration. More ideas. It is about working in sync with the Universe.

Maybe you have an idea that excites you so much, you do find a way to work ten times more powerfully. But because it is something you are passionate about, it doesn't feel like work. It feels exhilarating. You are happy to get up in the morning, excited to start your day. You're eager to see what unfolds in the hours ahead.

Remember that the easiest way to allow more abundance in your life, and to shift your thinking to more allowing, is *step by step*. Building greater momentum takes time. You need to let past momentum – energy you already have been flowing on a frequency that was not so allowing – play out. It will eventually become exhausted, especially as you no longer activate it. Because continuing to pay attention to something feeds its energy and keeps building it.

Like a car in motion that needs time to slow down, your past momentum will eventually wear out. Do not be alarmed as you apply the principles in this book if you feel like you are encountering resistance. Because if a prosperity mindset is new to you, then you have created momentum from your past mindset of lack. And just as you are creating new momentum with your new thinking, momentum from your past patterns of thought will play out.

So build the new flow, the new momentum. And have fun doing it.

Just don't be surprised, or thrown off course, if some old momentum surfaces. Recognize it for what it is, and let it go.

Have you ever tried to push a car forward that's engine wasn't working? Maybe the car engine stops working while waiting at a traffic light, and you need to push the car to the side of the road, out of the way of other vehicles. At first, it is hard to get that car moving. But then it picks up speed. It is easier to *keep* the car moving than to *start* it moving from a place of inertia.

If you have abundance energy that feels slowed down from an inertia of lack, it may take a while to build speed and increase the flow and movement of abundance.

The most important, lasting change is always in the vibration you are offering. In your frequency.

So if you have been offering a frequency of lack for a really long time, and some money comes, you may want to park the money somewhere safe until you have achieved a higher frequency that you can trust.

Because you are the sole offerer of your vibration, you are also the only one who knows if you can trust what you are offering.

You know if it feels good. You know if it feels steady. You know if it feels like you have momentum on this new frequency.

When a car is pushed from a place of stasis into motion, the car still needs to be steered. It needs someone who is directing its movement.

You wouldn't add speed to a car when you could not control its direction. You wouldn't accelerate a car that is out of control.

Likewise, you want to feel that you have your vibrational frequency in alignment with what you want and where you want to go, before you accelerate it.

You would never drive a car down the road, and add speed to it while you simultaneously release control of the steering wheel. You would never say, "I just want to go really fast in this car and I don't care where it goes or what happens." Because you know that increased speed requires more focus, not less. Energy takes greater control and alignment when moving quickly.

So, back to the non-working car at the traffic light. You think about where you want that car to go *before* you start pushing. You create an *intentional direction* before you start moving the car. Particularly when you are working with others to push the car, it is important you are working together. Your combined efforts will move the car faster – but only if you are all pushing in the same direction. If your energies are not focused on the same goal, it can require more effort and you can create resistance for each other.

Your thoughts and your energies need to be focused on moving forward. You want direction *before* you start pushing.

You know you want more. You want the car to gain speed. But in what direction do you want to go?

It may help to stay general in your initial thoughts. But do spend time developing the vision you would like to steer your life toward.

Have you ever met people who, even in their 20's, are saving for retirement? Financial security is a goal. They may already have a dollar amount in mind they hope – and plan – to have saved when they retire. They are clear with a long-term vision, and likely follow it up with a long-term plan.

Does it mean that they will always be able to stick to that plan? Of course not. Maybe their life takes a different turn. Or maybe even a better, more fun direction.

But do think about your future. Do develop a vision. Develop a sense of direction for where you want to steer your car before it builds up speed. Create focus for the flow of energy you are allowing so that you have clarity of direction as you channel it.

Chapter 60: It's Only Money

When you are feeling a great financial lack, money can seem like the most important thing on earth.

But it's not.

Humans existed for hundreds of thousands of years before money even came into being.

Earth has existed for billions of years.

The bartering of things, animals and services was important to human economy long before the first coins were ever created.

And today, more and more money is changing hands electronically, without people ever holding it in their physical hands.

There are all kinds of wealth. Financial wealth is only one aspect to experience. And many would argue it is not the worthiest kind.

Relationships matter more. A sense of self-worth and self-fulfillment. Happiness. The people and animals you love, who love you.

And the many things that humans create in their lives, from businesses to works of art and literature to vehicles to homes and families.

Money has not played a large role in society until recently, historically speaking.

But relationships have been crucial for billions of years.

Now, that may not mean much to you if you have past due bills and creditors calling.

But when people take money *too* seriously, it can produce shortage.

When you magnify what you are feeling about money with an intensity brought on by a sense of lack, then the shortage can multiply instead of the prosperity you are seeking.

So what we are saying essentially is: lighten up about money.

Lighten up how you are feeling about it, how you are thinking about it.

Don't let it be the most important thing in your life, whether you have it in abundance or not.

Perhaps you have heard someone comment, "It's only money."

And if you are feeling a tremendous shortage of money, it feels like a cruel statement. "How could anyone say that," you might wonder, "when lack can cause such pain?"

But many of the nations with the happiest people in the world are not the most financially prosperous. Because being happy matters more than money. Having money doesn't affect every moment of your day – but how you feel does.

A feeling of heaviness around the topic of money – which is often what people experiencing shortage have – is actually resistance that can keep you from attracting money into your life. It blocks the flow, and your receptivity.

It's like going to the grocery store with twenty dollars. If you feel that twenty dollars has to last you a long time, you are very careful with what you buy. Every cent matters.

But it you know there is more coming, or is already available, then you just purchase what you need or want without as much consideration of the price of each item.

If you have to feed the baby and the dog and you with that twenty dollars, then you likely feel a need to be cautious and perhaps a bit creative to see how far you can stretch them.

That's not feeling easy about money, or like you can trust its flow.

You may shift between gratitude for the twenty dollars, and having the feeling that it's *only* twenty dollars.

But you could be in the same situation, and talk yourself into a better feeling place.

At least you have the twenty dollars.

And at least you have the baby and dog with whom to spend time and share love. Those feelings of love and togetherness can be quite rewarding. You have each other.

You still need to eat. Food is vital. But maybe money isn't the most important thing after all.

A lot of people laugh and enjoy life – without a lot of money.

People with a lot of money may – or may not – be laughing.

So...why are we trying to shake up your values here?

Because we want you to value your own happiness.

We want you to value the relationships that exist in your life, independent of your financial situation.

We want you to value the feeling of fulfillment you get, and the meaning that fulfillment brings to your life.

We want you to value what you create, and the fun you have in creating – whether it is telling a story to a child, decorating a canvas or the place you live, or building an empire.

The lighter you feel about money, the easier you allow it to flow. And the more you *do not impede the natural flow of abundance to you*.

Given the structure of modern society, money may be an important part of how you live the life you want.

But it doesn't have to feel like it is the most important thing.

For millions of years, to humans and their ancestors, it hasn't been the most important thing.

In the past, the survival of the human species – of any species – was not dependent on money.

And many might argue that money has caused the elimination of numerous species, more than the creation of new ones.

So place money within its broader context. Give it a new perspective in your life.

It is only one aspect of living. Of thriving.

Maybe right now, it is an important aspect. But what is most important to you – really – in your life?

Can you be resourceful and create happiness, regardless of your financial situation?

Can you learn to laugh without lots of money in your bank account? (Or maybe even without a bank account?)

Financial prosperity is only one kind of prosperity. Financial abundance is only one kind of abundance, in a world where many things are abundant.

Allow the concept of money to find balance in your life with everything else that matters to you.

Money may be a part of the picture, but it is only a part of the broader picture of your life.

Consider the meaning that you want to assign it.

Chapter 61: My Abundance Now

Take a few moments and make a list of the abundance that is in your life now – the abundance that feels good, that you can appreciate and be happy about.

I am experiencing abundance right now.

I already have abundance in my life in so many ways.

Here are some examples. Take what works for you from this list. Then add more. Personalize it. Make it your own!

Examples:

I have an abundance of friends.

I have an abundance of family members and relatives.

I have an abundance of amazing animals.

I have an abundance of positive relationships.

I have an abundance of interesting things to do.

I have an abundance of good foods available to me.

I have an abundance of activities I enjoy.

I have an abundance of nature around me.

I have an abundance of flowers, trees, bushes, grasses that I can enjoy every day.

I have an abundance of concrete, steel, glass and metal that remind me how creative and industrious people are.

I can look onto an abundance of sky and clouds every day.

I have an abundance of appliances that make my life easier.

I have an abundance of stores available to me with products that are convenient.

I have an abundance of vehicles in my community that remind me how mobile people enjoy being.

I have an abundance of books and other reading/listening materials available to me in the library or on the internet.

I have an abundance of music available to me.

I have an abundance of engaging and uplifting programs and videos to view through television or online.

I have an abundance of knowledge easily accessible to me.

I have an abundance of ideas.

I have an abundance of thoughts.

I have an abundance of desires.

I have an abundance of accomplishments and tasks I have completed.

I have an abundance of successes.

I have an abundance of love...to give and to allow in.

I have an abundance of times I have been helpful to others.

I have an abundance of times others have been helpful to me.

I have an abundance of times I worked in partnership or teams with others to accomplish things.

I have an abundance of good memories, and I am making more all the time.

I am experiencing abundance right now.

Chapter 62: Making Friends with Abundance

If you were to draw a picture of abundance, what would it look like?

Would it be beautiful? Would it be glorious? Would you want to hang it in your home?

If you were to draw a picture of your relationship with money, would it be kind? Vibrant? Loving? Engaging?

What colors would you use?

Then ask yourself, "What would I like a picture to look like, if I were to draw a picture of the relationship *I desire* with abundance?"

How would that picture – of the relationship you desire – be different from the relationship you have right now?

In other words, are you friends with abundance?

Are you friends with money?

Sometimes, when young children draw pictures of family and friends, they are standing close to each other. It is obvious they like each other. Maybe they are hugging or engaged in a fun activity together. Perhaps the sun is shining in the background.

Would you and abundance even be on the same page? Would you be standing close to each other? Would it be clear that you like each other?

Would you be having fun together?

Would you and abundance be standing hand in hand?

Would you and money be smiling?

Would there be a big sun in the sky?

It's important to make friends with abundance. With prosperity. With money.

And as silly as it may sound, a child's drawing is a great way to begin because it goes back to basics.

"We like each other.

We have fun together.

We're happy together.

The sun smiles on us."

Now, if you think all of this is silly, that's okay.

But sometimes, emotions can be made clear through even the simplest artwork.

You might make a collage – a happy collage of you and abundance. You and money. Full of good feelings about your friendship.

Friendship?

Yes. Because if there is something you want in your life, you need to be friends with it.

If there is something you desire, it helps to feel affection for it.

It helps to make the abstract more real.

Imagine you and money being great friends. "Hello, dear friend," you think as you receive income.

"Thanks for helping me spread the love," as you pay a bill.

Start thinking – and feeling – about money as you would a dear friend.

You are glad to see it. But you trust the longevity of your relationship. So even when you say goodbye, you know it's temporary. You will see each other again soon.

You feel a connection and that connection feels good.

Every time your friend shows up, you are happy to see your friend.

You feel fortunate to have this friend in your life.

You have faith in this friend. This is a reliable friend. This is a friend you trust to be there when needed – and for fun. You have lots of good times together too.

Consider what it would be like in your life to have money as a companion and friend.

Make friends with money. Bring it into your life with all the warmth and appreciation you feel for a real friend. And over time, as trust grows and develops, you will find you can depend on that friend more and more.

And eventually, in that picture of you and money, there is a huge sun – and it is always shining.

Chapter 63: Wrapping Up Your Gift to You

We sent this book to you because we understand your power of abundance. We want you to understand it, too.

You came to earth with a stream of well-being flowing to you. That stream of well-being includes abundance in many forms.

As you grew up, you learned – from those around you, perhaps from life circumstances – to turn down the flow, the stream coming from your non-physical faucet.

You have expressed a mighty desire to open it, and allow that flow to be strong and vibrant again.

We know you have the power to do that. We want you to know it, too.

Your first work is to allow. Allow the well-being to flow to you. Allow the abundance to flow to you.

Your second work is to cease thoughts that impede the flow, and focus instead on thoughts that allow the flow. No one can get in your way but you. There is no one to blame for the present or past. Let the past stay in the past. You have the power to create what you want in your life. You have the power to manifest the future you want. You have the power now. You always have.

Your third work is to embrace who you really are – the amazing, special, brilliant, powerful you. You are worthy and deserving of experiencing great abundance, and embracing all that you are. Believe it. Feel it. Know it.

Your fourth work is to expect improvement. Expect that things are getting better for you, easier for you. Expect that more abundance is already on its way to you. And trust in your ability to be in alignment with receiving it.

Expect inspiration about how you can create greater abundance in your life. And how you can open your faucet even more.

Expect that your life is getting better. And better. And better.

Let yourself feel the improvement now – even before it arrives in physical form. Energetically, it is already arriving. Energy precedes manifestation. If you can find the good feelings, then you know the physical manifestation is on its way. The good feelings *are* a manifestation.

Affirm that you are friends with money. And money is a friend of yours – one of your many friends.

Appreciate the abundance that is arriving in your life. And practice gratitude for what is there, because gratitude is a powerful affirmation.

Appreciate the flow of abundance. Because money, prosperity – these are just different forms of energy. Enjoying prosperity is like eating food – it is ongoing energy that helps to nourish you and support you thriving in your life.

Find joy. Then find more joy. And more. The happier you get, the easier it is for abundance to flow to you.

Find ease. Look around for the many ways there is ease in your life. Affirm it. Be grateful for it. And trust that greater ease is coming.

You have the power to create what you want. You have always had the power.

You thought you did. Now, you know you do.
The power is yours.

> **Notes** <

www.ingramcontent.com/pod-product-compliance
Lightning Source LLC
Chambersburg PA
CBHW021038090426
42738CB00006B/143